NEW DIRECTIONS FOR YOUTH DEVELOPMENT

Theory
Practice
Research

spring | 2010

and Creative Arts

Doris Sommer | *issue*
Andrés Sanín | *editors*

Gil G. Noam
Editor-in-Chief

JOSSEY-BASS™
An Imprint of
⟨W⟩WILEY

CULTURAL AGENTS AND CREATIVE ARTS
Doris Sommer, Andrés Sanín (eds.)
New Directions for Youth Development, No. 125, Spring 2010
Gil G. Noam, Editor-in-Chief
This is a peer-reviewed journal.

Microfilm copies of issues and articles are available in 16mm and 35mm, as well as microfiche in 105mm, through University Microfilms Inc., 300 North Zeeb Road, Ann Arbor, Michigan 48106-1346.

NEW DIRECTIONS FOR YOUTH DEVELOPMENT (ISSN 1533-8916, electronic ISSN 1537-5781) is part of The Jossey-Bass Psychology Series and is published quarterly by Wiley Subscription Services, Inc., A Wiley Company, at Jossey-Bass, 989 Market Street, San Francisco, California 94103-1741. POSTMASTER: Send address changes to New Directions for Youth Development, Jossey-Bass, 989 Market Street, San Francisco, California 94103-1741.

SUBSCRIPTIONS for individuals cost $85.00 for U.S./Canada/Mexico; $109.00 international. For institutions, agencies, and libraries, $249.00 U.S.; $289.00 Canada/Mexico; $323.00 international. Prices subject to change. Refer to the order form that appears at the back of most volumes of this journal.

EDITORIAL CORRESPONDENCE should be sent to the Editor-in-Chief, Dr. Gil G. Noam, McLean Hospital, Harvard Medical School, 115 Mill Street, Belmont, MA 02478.

Cover photograph by Pat Canova/Photolibrary
www.josseybass.com

Contents

Issue Editors' Notes

> When I feel trapped, I ask myself, what would an artist
> do?
>
> Antanas Mockus

"DON'T WORRY," SAID THE GRACIOUS FACILITATOR at the 2008
Medellín meeting of a UN-Habitat project to promote safer cities.
He was trying to assuage me after I had voiced concern about the
absence of art from the reports of experts, though the arts were
central in practically every example of progress in violence prevention among youth at risk. "Tomorrow," my accommodating
host continued, "we will spend the entire day with local youth leaders, and you'll see that all of them are artists." My worry dug in
deeper, of course, because the overwhelming evidence of creative
practices that channel unruliness into admirable products and performances had not yet made an impression on the experts who
came to discuss the safety and development of youth. Why would
more evidence matter if the researchers and advisers were filtering
out the available information about the efficacy of the arts? Prag-
matists know that data (about art, in this case) are not enough to
make an argument, because hard facts do not exist unless we notice
them, and noticing depends on culturally constructed expectations.[1]
All seventeen of the international experts who gathered in September 2008 to consider best practices and good bets for future
policy apparently had little expectation that art mattered for youth
development, or they avoided any mention of the arts, as if playful
and unconventional expression were light fare, unworthy of
weighty consideration.

Inspired by the efforts and the effectiveness of Medellín's collaboration with youth leaders, I felt moved on the first day to observe, aloud, that it was no coincidence to find that these leaders were artists: specifically rappers, graffiti artists, break dancers, actors. Art, after all, enables the kind of empowerment that the experts were prescribing for the population they called "youth at risk." Offering sound bites from aesthetic theory, I mentioned that art defamiliarizes the practices and surroundings that we hardly notice anymore out of habit. From the most intimate everyday routines to the most public catastrophes, habit breeds indifference even to danger and to death as we anticipate repetition, and we hardly register repetition as noteworthy. The function of art is to intervene in order to upset conventional patterns, to create surprise in situations that had seemed familiar and unremarkable. Interventions refresh perception as well as one's performance in society. Viktor Shklovsky formulated this characteristic of art early in the twentieth century. Art, he was sure, has nothing to do with content, but everything to do with technique. It is an interruption of expectations that rekindles a love for the world, reviving objects, events, and people deadened by habit. Without art, "life is reckoned as nothing. Habitualization devours works, clothes, furniture, one's wife, and the fear of war. . . . And art exists that one may recover the sensation of life."[2]

This lesson from Russian formalism bears on both consumers and producers of art. But producers represent a greater good to society because they multiply the instances and therefore the life-affirming effects of art. Artists create the added value of channeling nonconformist energies toward productive practices, so they do not fester and explode into violence. In any genre, art thrives on contradiction and struggle.[3] Making something new depends on that struggle, so that creative activities acknowledge the frustrating straits that youth at risk experience. They also deflect frustration from potentially damaging responses into aesthetic challenges that sometimes produce beautiful results. In the best cases for society, art can lead to economic and civic gains. The double

NEW DIRECTIONS FOR YOUTH DEVELOPMENT • DOI: 10.1002/yd

duty of art is captured brilliantly in the slogan for Toronto's art center called Remix Project: "Make money. Make Change."

The participating psychologists, political scientists, policy experts, urban planners, lawyers, and international functionaries at the next session of our meeting generally mustered their well-meaning talents and dedication toward reaching useful conclusions from examples and from reflection so that next steps might follow. The serious reflection would lead to at least one positive next step: a meeting at Harvard University in 2009 between the Cultural Agents Initiative and the Safer Cities project to develop an arts module in the work of violence prevention.

The following day, we did indeed spend our time with youth leaders in the Comuna 13, underneath the cable cars of Medellín's airlift transportation system. The morning saw us walking up a steep street bordered by probably unauthorized but rather decent construction when, to our surprise and delight, the children's walking band broke out into a musical welcome. At the top of the street, on the top of their community center that features clubs in theater, poetry, painting, and instrumental music among other arts often supported by municipal contributions, the youth of Son Batá regaled us with first-rate performances. Leaders were former combatants who had trained the neighborhood youth in hip-hop arts and in a tangent back to the traditional rhythms and playful lyrics from the youths' heritage Afro-Colombian Pacific coastal area of Chocó. It was a general invitation to participate, and chairs piled up alongside the rooftop forum to give visitors and hosts some space to dance together.

I was impressed by the multiarts design of the collective that engaged all the young people whatever their individual talents and passions and congratulated the youth leaders for constructing the principle of multiple intelligences on the ground. Added to the performance creativity was their entrepreneurial drive to produce, market, and promote the arts. The cluster of activities inspired me to imagine that they could constitute a model "Cartonera Crew" to multiply Cultural Agents' multiarts literacy program called La cartonera (also known as Paper Picker Press, PPP). With origins in Sarita Cartonera of Lima, Peru, the program uses literary classics as raw material for new works created by children and youth. Participants receive instruction from a range of artists who rotate through the classrooms or youth groups to teach techniques for interpreting the literary text through painting, dance, music, photography, and other arts. Young people become "authors" of their variations on classic works; they come to own those works as they develop high-level language competence and higher-order thinking to interpret and develop existing material. The PPP is being adapted to local settings, with attention to local literary traditions and local artists in several countries and at home in the Boston area. Among our partners is the Young People's Project, which teaches math literacy through games and arts to inner-city children by employing inner-city youth as facilitators.

"Would you be interested in adding literature, challenging classics of literature, to your mix," I asked, "so that all the other arts would interpret the text and thereby teach literacy at a high level through artistic play?" They were in fact interested and made plans to join a training session the next month in Bogotá. Like the rappers who had spun Shakespeare for performances at the Strand Theater in the Dorchester neighborhood of Boston, these hip-hop artists already knew how to turn the pope's sermon, or a historic speech by Gaitán, into rap. One attraction of the "Cartonera Crew," they understood, would be economic solvency for the artists once schools hired the arts collective to enhance programs of language arts. At present, bands and dancers compete with each other in the limited market of concerts, record sales, and T-shirt design. Resources for education might support more artists and mitigate competition. But the main attraction, of course, is the superior education in reading, writing, and critical thinking that the youth leaders could provide to children through the Paper Picker Press/Cartonera. (See culturalagents.org; go to Programs; then to Paper Picker Press/Cartonera.)

In one of the stellar articles in this volume, "Thinking Creatively Is Thinking Critically," Elizabeth Gruenfeld highlights the aim to promote the celebration of language, culture, and creativity through collaboration between great writers and cardboard collectors. In both Buenos Aires and Lima, the projects produced and published beautiful books with hand-painted cardboard covers that speak of the excellent literature inside. With such works, the communities of Buenos Aires produced income for the poorest residents; in Lima, the works inspired teachers and their students, fostering a new and profound appreciation of literature and creativity in the community. By responding to their national circumstances, both Cartonera programs bring their national fictions into reality by literally rewriting the historical situation of their nations and communities.

Exemplary initiatives like this one, like the Young People's Project, the Son Batá, and other youth-centered arts programs featured in this volume, foreground the crucial role that arts play in youth development. The arts value youthful nonconformity and divergent thinking as foundations of art rather than proposing to enforce restrictions on that energy or to describe it as socially pathological. These exemplary creative practices should spark recognition of the agency of art in other existing or potential initiatives that merit our attention and support. One measure of our support will be to incorporate creative practices in our own interpretation and teaching. The point is worth underlining in order to connect the intrinsic value of art as escape from deadening habit to the added value of humanist commentary and interpretation that we teach in school and out of school. Like writers, composers, painters, and playwrights, teachers who help students interpret art can also train youth to explore divergent points of view and admire variations and interpretations that come from other classmates. Rather than merely tolerating fellow participants and acknowledging that people feel and think differently, even beyond culturally determined patterns, youth who develop arts and interpretation learn to appreciate the variety of interventions in a shared text as contributions to their own enriched enjoyment of art and of social engagements. So much depends on the delicacy and skill of interpretation that often determines the pleasure and after-effects of art works. "There is nothing either good or bad," says the artist Shakespeare, "but thinking makes it so" (*Hamlet*, II:2).

Teachers are agents of culture who multiply the lessons they learn by reaching masses of students, whatever the reigning taste in art may be. To make good on this broad-based power of persuasion, teachers and youth leaders may want to add a reflexive question to lesson plans: How does our pedagogical work affect the world? In fact, all of us are cultural agents: those who make, comment, buy, sell, reflect, allocate, decorate, vote, do not vote, or otherwise lead social, culturally constructed lives. The appropriate question about agency is not if we exercise it but how self-consciously we do so—that is, to what end and what effect.

Agent is a term that acknowledges the small shifts in perspective and practice that can turn artists and teachers into first movers toward collective change.[4] The option of agency releases youth from the familiar double-bind of expecting too much from art and too little. On the one hand, artists and critics can make the radical and impractical demand that art replace a bad social system for a better one; on the other, they may stop short of expecting any change and stay stuck in denunciation, irony, cynicism, melancholy. Between frustrated ambition and helplessness, agency is a modest but relentless call to creative action, one small step at a time.[5] It enables artists, young and old, to engage the existing social world instead of either discarding it or despairing altogether (personal communication with Pedro Reyes, June 8, 2005).

The articles that follow suggest the range of possible cultural agents, and they will surely trigger the reader's recognition of local cultural agents who add their own inspirations to stimulate creative interventions by youth. To intervene is to recognize that situations are given, materials exist in particular arrangements of scarcity or excess, and cultural patterns interpret these contexts and materials in predictable, habitual ways. But existing situations are not necessarily static; they show gaps or fissures that allow for artful interventions.

In "More Carrots Than Sticks: Antanas Mockus's Civic Culture Policy in Bogotá," Felipe Cala Buendía recounts the accomplishments of a mayor who engaged the youth of what was then the most chaotic and corrupt city in the Americas to rescue civility through a combined program of arts and institutional reform. Mayor Mockus invited the youth to develop weekly concerts, known as Rock in the Park, and reclaim public space even at night; he hosted art contests for AIDS prevention, and staged performances of youth emerging from empty gravesites to celebrate the dramatic reduction of homicides during his administration.

In "Voicing Differences: Indigenous and Urban Radio in Argentina, Chile, and Nigeria," Luis E. Cárcamo-Huechante and Nicole Delia Legnani highlight the contributions of young programmers and technicians who promote indigenous cultures throughout the Americas and the rest of the world through radio waves. The programs maintain home languages; provide access to health, education, and employment information; greet friends and relatives; and recreate traditional culture under circumstances of modern pressures and opportunities.

Iberia Pérez González adds the power of visual arts in "Silent Gains: Instituto Buena Bista and Art as Catalyst Among Curaçaoan Youth." The center for contemporary visual art in the Dutch Caribbean island of Curaçao has been strongly committed to promoting the practice and value of painting, drawing, and sculpture and to providing an outlet for Curaçaoan youth who can channel their creative and sometimes provocative energies into developing their imagination and creative skills. The research reported in this article demonstrates that initiatives in art education can act as catalysts in the formation of social agents, not only by fostering an alternative approach to general education through the visual arts but, most important, by affording vehicles to turn youthful experimentation into productive forms of citizenship.

Elaine L. Wang's "The Beat of Boyle Street: Empowering Aboriginal Youth Through Music Making" develops the potential of sonic arts to literally give voice to indigenous youth. Aboriginal youth in Canada continue to be marginalized and to run higher risks than white counterparts. They have low school attendance rates and high dropout rates. They tend to be poor, even homeless,

NEW DIRECTIONS FOR YOUTH DEVELOPMENT • DOI: 10.1002/yd

and prey to drugs and alcohol, gangs, and criminal activity. In 2003, The Beat of Boyle Street was founded to reconnect this population of youth to school and help them establish a healthy sense of self. The medium is rap and remixes, using technology to record and produce their own music. The Beat of Boyle Street has won awards and accolades. It is a successful program that can be adapted and applied elsewhere to empower other at-risk youth groups.

In every sense of the word, Marco A. Abarca is the author of Aula Verde, a green classroom in Puerto Rico. He is a creative Costa Rican human rights lawyer who had been called on to consult about an ongoing class action lawsuit against unconstitutional prison conditions in Puerto Rico. Abarca, now a law professor at the University of Puerto Rico, managed to direct part of the fine monies accumulated throughout years of litigation toward an investment that would improve living conditions in one of the largest and poorest housing projects in Puerto Rico. Together with community participants, consisting of many young parolees and probationers, Abarca began to transform the mosquito-infested badland behind a Catholic school into a natural haven. Then, with the help of science educators, the group designed a workshop for elementary school children on urban ecology. As the participants organized, what developed was a community-based, self-employed enterprise known as Aula Verde. Its expert workshops are certified by the Department of Education of Puerto Rico and supported with Title 1 funds for the approximately twelve thousand elementary school children who visit each year. By now the concept of Aula Verde is an inspiration for other consolidated sustainable development initiatives that can significantly improve lives in marginalized communities and at the same time enhance the education of Puerto Rico's youth.

"Fill in the Blank: Culture Jamming and the Advertising of Agency" by Carrie Lambert-Beatty reflects on the power of talking back through visual images, a creative intervention that engages the spirit of hip-hop and the practices of young artists. What she calls "billboard liberation" contests conventional advertising in a playful and youthful way. In one of her examples, Ji Lee's Bubble

Project, an artist places blank thought-bubble stickers on street advertisements and waits to see what people write on them, completing the work of art and transgression. There are other interesting initiatives from the collective Illegal Art, like one in which blank pages with the word *God* were placed around the city in place of advertising, inviting people to complete the prayer/complaint and participate in a Suggestion Box, a ludic project that collected "suggestions" from people out in the street. All of these artistic initiatives were pacific and joyful ways to "rebel" toward the impositions of powers such as media and advertising that could be related to the rebel spirit of adolescence.

In "Technepolitics: Who Has a Stake in the Making of an American Identity?" Christina Suszynski Green adds to our appreciation of the distinguished Puerto Rican artist Antonio Martorell by underlining his collaborations with youth. Despite having just celebrated his seventieth birthday, the maestro Martorell is a child in spirit, who explores in many playful ways the infinite possibilities of art such as engaging the youth in Ponce, Puerto Rico, and in Boston in his workshops and in creative dialogues and artistic adventures. In one collaboration they create a mosaic path into the sea, and in another they made "carbon copies" of the classics at Harvard's Fogg Museum.

The collaborative contribution by David M. Washington and Devin G. Beecher, "Music as Social Medicine: Two Perspectives on the West-Eastern Divan Orchestra," offers a leitmotif of music therapy for social stagnation. In the Middle Eastern version, Israeli and Arab youth meet in Spain and throughout the rest of the world to practice and play together. And in the "El Sistema," Venezuela's poorest youth have broad access to classical music through youth orchestras created thirty years ago by the composer and economist Antonio Abreu. The program is living proof of the power of music and education to generate social change on a great scale. The project has integrated 120 youth orchestras from that country, transforming the lives of many children, including Gustavo Dudamel, its most famous graduate, who has directed orchestras such as the Israel Philharmonic and the Los Angeles Philharmonic. This initiative was recently awarded the prize of Príncipe de Asturias de las Artes and has inspired many others around the world, such as one in Providence, Rhode Island, and one in Cali, Colombia.

Maria Tereza Schaedler is lucky enough to have studied directly with Augusto Boal. In "Boal's Theater of the Oppressed and How to Derail Real-Life Tragedies with Imagination," she shares her own expertise as a practicing artist and educator of youth and adult immigrants. In the 1960s Boal created a process whereby audience members could stop a performance and suggest alternative lines and gestures for the actors. Taking the interventions a step further, he began inviting audience members onto the stage to demonstrate their ideas. In so doing, he discovered that through this participation, the audience becomes empowered not only to imagine change but also to practice that change and thereby generate social action. For Boal this was the birth of the "spect-actor" (not spectator), and his theater was transformed. His techniques are practiced worldwide among all sectors of society, including many youth activists.

We hope that these inspiring cases will encourage leaders of youth groups and their participants to imagine their own creative and constructive interventions in nagging problems through artful practices that amount to social contributions. From a mayor who managed to revive an apparently hopeless city, to indigenous voices that defend precarious cultures on radio waves, and convicts who commute their sentences by serving as instructors in a green classroom, among many other engaging accounts, the cultural agents featured here can be mentors for youth who would develop their own sense of authorship and agency.

Doris Sommer
Editor

Notes

1. Rorty, R. (2007). *Philosophy as cultural politics*. Cambridge: Cambridge University Press.

2. Shklovsky, V. (1965). Art as technique. In *Russian formalist criticism: Four essays* (pp. 3–24). Lincoln: University of Nebraska Press.

3. Schiller, F. (1967). *On the aesthetic education of man in a series of letters* (E. M. Wilkinson & L. A. Willoughby, Trans. and Eds.). New York: Oxford University Press. Also see Sommer, D. (2004). *Bilingual aesthetics: A new sentimental education.* Durham, NC: Duke University Press.

4. North, D. (1990). *Institutions, institutional change and economic performance.* Cambridge, MA: Harvard University Press; North, D. (1990). A transaction cost theory of politics. *Journal of Theoretical Politics, 2,* 355–367.

5. Sommer, D. "Wiggle room." In *Cultural agency in the Americas.* Durham, NC: Duke University Press, 2006.

DORIS SOMMER *is the Ira and Jewell Williams Professor of Romance Languages and Literatures, and of African and African American Studies at Harvard University; she is also director of Cultural Agents.*

Executive Summary

Chapter One: More carrots than sticks: Antanas Mockus's civic culture policy in Bogotá

Felipe Cala Buendía

The son of a Lithuanian artist, Antanas Mockus was the president of the National University in Colombia before he became mayor of Bogotá in 1995. As mayor, he transformed the city into a huge classroom, not only bringing to his administration a new view of governing but also transforming the way people exercised their citizenship. Mockus resorted to a creative communicative and pedagogical effort to change the citizens' hearts and minds in favor of peaceful coexistence and legal compliance. Symbols, metaphors, and humor became the language through which the administration would enforce its measures to deal with urban violence. Unconventional techniques, such as a symbolic vaccine against domestic violence and the use of mimes to control traffic circulation and create a sense of shame among those who committed infractions, helped to stop crime and develop a new sense of citizenship.

Chapter Two: Voicing differences: Indigenous and urban radio in Argentina, Chile, and Nigeria

Luis E. Cárcamo-Huechante, Nicole Delia Legnani

Indigenous cultures throughout the Americas and the rest of the world have to deal with problems of cultural assimilation, migration,

NEW DIRECTIONS FOR YOUTH DEVELOPMENT, NO. 125, SPRING 2010 © WILEY PERIODICALS, INC.
Published online in Wiley InterScience (www.interscience.wiley.com) • DOI: 10.1002/yd.334

and dissemination of their populations. Some of them, in countries such as Argentina, Chile, and Nigeria, have developed radio programming to maintain home languages; gain access to health, education, and employment information; greet friends and relatives; and re-create traditional culture under circumstances of modern pressures but also to open up opportunities. This article explores the capacity and awareness of these contributions in a multicultural world.

Chapter Three: Silent gains: Instituto Buena Bista and art as catalyst among Curaçaoan youth

Iberia Pérez González

Considering the limited opportunities and resources for creative education, artists David Bade and Tirzo Martha, along with art historian Nancy Hoffmann, developed a dynamic platform to support creative young talent on the Dutch Caribbean island of Curaçao. The aim of Instituto Buena Bista (IBB), founded in 2006, is to strengthen the arena of culture and the visual arts by offering young Curaçaoans a basic but thorough course in art education that is meant to function as a springboard to more advanced art schools. With only two years of operation, the IBB is already seeing how some of its students go to art academies abroad and participate in art contests in the Netherlands. An exploration of how the IBB is filling up a cultural void by proposing an alternative to local youth education that allows them to develop a *buena bista*—a new and different view of their island, their futures, and themselves.

Chapter Four: The Beat of Boyle Street: Empowering Aboriginal youth through music making

Elaine L. Wang

An irrepressibly popular musical phenomenon, hip-hop is close to spoken word and focuses on lyrics with a message, reviving local traditions of song that tell histories, counsel listeners, and challenge participants to outdo one another in clever exchanges. A hip-hop music-making program in Edmonton, Canada, successfully reengages at-risk Aboriginal youth in school with high levels of desertion and helps them establish a healthy sense of self and of their identity as Aboriginals.

Chapter Five: Thinking creatively is thinking critically
Elizabeth Gruenfeld

The Cartoneras projects aim to promote the celebration of language, culture, and creativity through a collaboration between top literary minds and cardboard collectors in Buenos Aires and Lima. They produce and publish beautiful books with hand-painted cardboard covers that speak of the wonderful literature inside. Inspired by those projects, the Paper Picker Press (PPP) program in Boston aims to engage higher-order thinking through an arts-based approach to rediscovering literature through play. PPP starts with the premise that a student who is thinking creatively is also thinking critically. Creative play is critical thinking.

Chapter Six: Aula Verde: Art as experience in community-based environmental education
Marco A. Abarca

After winning a class-action lawsuit against unconstitutional prison conditions in Puerto Rico, Marco Abarca managed to direct part of the fine monies accumulated throughout years of litigation toward an investment that would improve the living conditions in one of the largest and poorest housing projects in Puerto Rico. With the participation of parolees and probationers, he began to transform a mosquito-infested badland into a natural haven. Then, with the help of science educators, the group designed a workshop for elementary school children on urban ecology. As the participants organized, what developed was a community-based, self-employed enterprise known as Aula Verde.

Chapter Seven: Fill in the blank: Culture jamming and the advertising of agency

Carrie Lambert-Beatty

This article is a review on billboard liberation and some other projects that develop the idea of talking back or over advertising in a playful and youthful way. In one of them, Ji Lee's Bubble Project, an artist places blank thought-bubble stickers on street advertisements and waits to see what people write on them, completing the work of art and transgression. In other initiative, blank pages with the word *God* were placed around the city in place of advertising, inviting people to complete the prayer/complaint and to participate in a Suggestion Box, a project that collected "suggestions" from people out in the street. A review of playful and youthful ways to "rebel" against the impositions of powers like media and advertising.

Chapter Eight: Technepolitics: Who has a stake in the making of an American identity?

Christina Suszynski Green

Following the lineage of Taller Alacrán, the workshop of Puerto Rican maestro Antonio Martorell, the author explores the studio workshop model as an alternative or a supplement to public school arts education models. Arguing that the production of art is a means of making one's ideas or one's community visible and that the inability, whether through education or funds, to create art can silence a person or a community, she questions whether the government is the most appropriate steward of urban public school students' arts education, given its track record of silencing artists

with the reduction and removal of funds. The article offers rec-
ommendations to education professionals based on the Taller
Alacrán studio system.

Chapter Nine: Music as social medicine: Two perspectives on the West-Eastern Divan Orchestra

David M. Washington, Devin G. Beecher

The social power of music can effect stable and positive changes in
individual health and communities that have significant health risks.
Two observers, a medical student and a music student, discuss
respectively the ideals and challenges of this principle put into practice. Their reflections about the role of music as social therapy and
space for cultural communication stem from their one-week
involvement with the West-Eastern Divan Orchestra at its summer
institute in Spain.

Chapter Ten: Boal's Theater of the Oppressed and how to derail real-life tragedies with imagination

Maria Tereza Schaedler

In the 1960s, Augusto Boal created a process whereby audience
members could stop a performance and suggest different actions
for the actors, who would then carry out the audience's suggestions.
Then, he began inviting audience members onto the stage to
demonstrate their ideas and discovered that through their participation they become empowered not only to imagine change but
also to practice it and generate social action. The author studied
with him and shares with us her own expertise as a practicing artist
and educator of youth and adult immigrants, using Boal's revolutionary methods.

In 1995, Bogotá was one of the most violent and dangerous cities in the world. That was when Mayor Antanas Mockus decided to use pedagogical and artful initiatives as policy tools to turn things around.

1

More carrots than sticks: Antanas Mockus's civic culture policy in Bogotá

Felipe Cala Buendía

IN 1993, THE PRESIDENT of the National University in Colombia, Antanas Mockus, dropped his pants and mooned a rowdy student audience in order to silence them. The episode, broadcast that night as part of the evening news, not only catapulted Mockus into the country's public scene, but also revealed to that same public the unusual and eccentric character of his methods. This would be but the first of his many theatrical displays, for soon after, Mockus resigned his post and decided to run for mayor of Bogotá. Although he lacked political experience, Mockus became an electoral success in a country where traditional politics was extremely discredited. And in 1994, he was elected to the country's second most important public office.

I received useful comments on earlier drafts of this article from my colleagues at Princeton University, Elena Peregrina-Salvador and Matthew Tremé. Andrés Sanín and Doris Sommer, from Harvard University, were more than generous in their reactions to the text. My gratitude goes to all of them. Remaining infelicities, grammatical and substantive, are mine alone.

Bogotá was then one of the most dangerous and ungovernable cities in Latin America. Nevertheless, Mockus stepped up to the challenge and soon turned the city into a social experiment, implementing a series of initiatives aimed at promoting peaceful coexistence and legal compliance among the citizenry. This wide range of initiatives, all brought together under the rubric of civic culture (*cultura ciudadana*), included such diverse measures as controlling the most salient risk factors for violence, namely the consumption of alcohol and the bearing of firearms; reconfiguring the institutional setting for policy formulation and implementation; strengthening the metropolitan police; and fundamentally redressing the way citizens interacted with each other, the authorities, and the city.

The objective of this initiative was to bestow the responsibility of dealing with violence not only on the authorities (in charge of enforcing the law) but also on individual citizens (in charge of complying with it in favor of the common good). Thus, Mockus embraced his role as an educator, not only bringing to his administration a new view of governing but also transforming the way people exercised their citizenship. To effect this transformation, Mockus resorted to a creative communicative and pedagogical effort to change the citizens' hearts and minds in favor of peaceful coexistence and legal compliance. Symbols, metaphors, and humor became the language through which the administration would enforce its measures to deal with urban violence. This new approach, principally aimed at educating the citizenry, coincided with a change in the city's violence during the three years of the Mockus administration. The annual homicide rate dropped from 69.69 to 47.08 homicides per 100,000 people and the number of homicides from 3,385 to 2,614.[1]

Between 1995 and 1997, after having been considered one of the most dangerous cities in the Americas, why did Bogotá experience a decrease in violence? Throughout the ensuing years, several arguments have been brought forth in order to answer this question, including those that speak of a national trend, an increase in sanctions against criminals, an improvement of socioeconomic conditions, or institutional enhancement.[2] Although I believe that no single factor can account for an increase or a decrease in violence, this being a multifaceted phenomenon, it is my contention that one of the intervening factors in Bogotá's experience lies in the implementation of the civic culture policy, and more specifically in a set of measures—artful, creative, and eccentric as they were—aimed at redressing the way citizens interacted with each other, the authorities, and the city.

This article assesses the impact of Mockus's communicative and pedagogical efforts and ventures a hypothesis to explain such an impact. For even if the drop in the city's homicide rate has been widely acknowledged as a meaningful experience in terms of urban governance, mainly because of the figures themselves, there are no explanations as to why the civic culture policy managed to have an impact on the behavior of citizens.[3] Ultimately I hint at the relevance of this sort of experiment as part of the wide array of policy options to address urban violence.

I approach Mockus's civic culture program as a set of policy initiatives that, besides their occasional eccentricity or even outright wackiness, are part and parcel of an ambitious philosophical and social project. I first present what I consider to be the most relevant creative measures implemented during the first Mockus administration (1995–1997): the so-called Temperance Law (*Ley Zanahoria*), the voluntary disarmament campaigns, and the two vaccination campaigns against violence. I also present some of the results yielded by these initiatives as a way to assess their impact on the drop in the city's homicide rate. Second, I identify what I believe to be the most salient factors, among others, to account for this impact: Mockus's leadership and the agentive power of creativity and the arts as fundamental components of the civic culture policy.[4]

A new approach to Bogotá's urban violence

In 1995, several municipal agencies got together to draft Bogotá's development plan for the next three years. Civic culture was recognized as one of its six priorities and became one of the articulating categories that would determine the city's spending during Mockus's incumbency. Here, the concept at hand was defined as "the ensemble of customs, activities, and shared minimum rules intended to create a feeling of belonging, facilitate urban coexistence, and produce respect for collective goods and recognition of citizens' rights and duties."[5]

To achieve its purposes, the civic culture policy encompassed a wide range of legal measures and communicative initiatives, often involving creativity and the arts, all aimed at engineering a change in the way citizens interacted with each other, the authorities, and the city. These initiatives were conceived as a series of concrete measures and actions to prevent those events and circumstances considered to induce or trigger violent behavior: the misuse of alcohol, the bearing of firearms, and violence within the family. All of these measures were especially aimed at young people as a way to redress the way they behaved and interacted in public spaces.

Arguably the most controversial measure undertaken by the Mockus administration was the Temperance Law, which was intended to reduce the number of alcohol-related deaths in the city. Forensic data has revealed to the administration the close relationship between alcohol consumption and violence. In 1995, most of the violent deaths in Bogotá took place late at night and mostly over the weekends.[6] Furthermore, alcohol was involved in 49 percent of traffic accidents, in 33 percent of homicides committed with firearms, and in 49 percent of those committed with knives.[7] With these figures, it was evident that something had to be done.

Thus, in accordance with the Temperance Law, implemented in December 1995, no alcohol could be sold in Bogotá after 1:00 A.M. In addition, bars, clubs, and restaurants that offered alcoholic drinks were required to close at this hour. Roadblocks and police enforcement were boosted, and sanctions against drunk drivers were drastically increased. However, due to the resistance not only of bar and restaurant owners, but also of youths and young adults, the administration was required to undertake an aggressive campaign to underscore the importance of this measure and commu-

NEW DIRECTIONS FOR YOUTH DEVELOPMENT • DOI: 10.1002/yd

nicate its intent and alleged results.[8] Such initiatives ranged from the symbolic display of giant carrots at the mayor's office to shocking television ads, and a series of alcohol-awareness lectures, in which more than thirty-five hundred teenage students participated.[9] Among them, 79 percent declared being more aware of the dangers of alcohol consumption, and 57 percent reported a change in their alcohol consumption practices.[10]

Those same data led the Mockus administration to control the bearing of firearms in the city, which included not only administrative and police measures but also an aggressive campaign to promote voluntary disarmament. Based on the fact that more than 70 percent of homicides in Bogotá involved a firearm, the administration launched an initiative in December 1996 through which people could exchange firearms and ammunition for Christmas gift cards.[11]

In this first campaign, 2,538 legal and illegal firearms, ammunition, and explosives were voluntarily surrendered.[12] By 2001 and through other similar initiatives, that figure had risen to over 6,500 firearms.[13] In the same way and by enhancing police control, the number of confiscated illegal firearms and weapons increased from 6,000 in 1995 to almost 16,000 in 2003.[14] All the weapons were melted and turned into tablespoons, each of them with an inscription that stated where it came from: "I was a firearm."[15]

Furthermore, and in accordance with the hypotheses that placed violence within the family—namely against women and children— at the core of the production of a culture of violence and a generalized tolerance for and trivialization of violent practices, the Mockus administration implemented what would become one of its most creative initiatives: the two vaccination campaigns against violence, which took place in 1996. More than a prevention strategy against violence within the family, this initiative was intended to sensitize the citizenry about this issue and, most important, its role in the reproduction of violence in general. During these events, a series of symbolic mechanisms were employed, with the aid of psychiatrists and psychologists, to allow victims of abuse to express their feelings toward their aggressor. Participants were asked to recall a past aggression or abuse, draw the features of the

NEW DIRECTIONS FOR YOUTH DEVELOPMENT • DOI: 10.1002/yd

perpetrator on a dummy, and verbally or physically express their feelings against it. At the end, victims were given a placebo as a symbolic vaccination against the reproduction of violence. More than forty-five thousand people participated in this initiative.[16]

The effects of the civic culture policy on the city's homicide rate are still a contested issue due to the lack of a comprehensive and complete set of data that would allow such an evaluation. However, a considerable number of students of this phenomenon regard these measures as an effective, and even exportable, means to address urban violence.[17] Furthermore, econometric analyses have argued that the measures to control the consumption of alcohol and the bearing of firearms can be said to account for 22 percent of the decrease in the city's homicide rate,[18] which fell from 58.91 to 39.04 per 100,000 people, between 1995 and 1999.[19]

Whether this impact is considered significant or merely marginal is not a matter of interest for the purposes of this article. My argument is that what is of foremost importance is that they had an effect: they constitute an intervening factor in the shift in the city's violence by changing the way citizens interacted with each other, the authorities, and the city.

Nevertheless, the way in which the authorities launched and promoted these initiatives exhibit certain particularities that go beyond the specificities of the Temperance Law, the voluntary disarmament campaign, or the vaccination campaigns against violence. These particularities refer to the incorporation of public health and epidemiology as effective ways of addressing urban violence, but also their combination with specific efforts to modify citizens' behavior through communication, educational and pedagogical activities, and artful interventions.

The agentive power of creativity and the arts

Although the impact of the civic culture policy can be explained through a whole range of factors—among them, the institutional setting of its implementation is of the foremost importance—my contention is that other factors are in play, and they are commonly overlooked by those who study this experience: the leadership exercised by the mayor himself and the agentive power of creativity and the arts.

In this respect, it is necessary to understand that Mockus appeared in the public sphere at a critical juncture in Colombia, one of extreme discrediting of traditional politics. This would explain why, with less than ten thousand dollars and in a country with strong political machineries, an independent candidate managed to win the election to Colombia's second most important public office, with 64.5 percent of the vote and breaking the Liberal and Conservative monopoly of power in the city.

As both a candidate and mayor, Mockus shook Bogotá's political arena not only through eccentric public displays like the one described at the beginning of this article, but also by introducing an innovative discourse in the exercise of political power itself. Creativity and the arts, as policy and pedagogical tools, would become the privileged ways in which his administration would communicate with the citizenry.

Humor and eccentricity, instead of coercion and top-down authority, gave way to an effective communication between the administration and its constituents. For example, in 1997, a water shortage hit the city. In accordance with the theoretical guidelines of the civic culture policy, Mockus implemented a campaign to promote saving water and to prevent restrictions in its supply by the official authorities. The strategy was one of intense communication. Each week, the mayor would report back to the citizenry the amount of water that had been saved. Furthermore, and very much in his style, he would appear on television shows while taking a shower; he would turn water off as he soaped and ask fellow citizens to do the same. However, as Cristina Rojas points out, communication went both ways. When water consumption increased by 2 percent at the end of the first week, the administration determined to find out why. When asked in a survey, citizens said they had been collecting water in case of a cut in the service. The administration reassured users and explained once again the whole purpose of reducing water consumption. In just two months, water consumption dropped by 14 percent and kept on dropping when people realized how much money they were saving due to the incentives approved by the Mockus administration.[20]

Although this story has little to do with urban violence, it is a good example of how Mockus managed to become an agent of change, setting a positive example and engaging in effective communication with his constituents, transforming the way they interacted with each other, the authorities, and the city, not only in terms of violent behavior but also in terms of everyday attitudes and practices.

Thus, in order to close the gap between the legal, moral, and cultural regulatory systems of human behavior, the Mockus administration directed its efforts at communicating and explaining the convenience of complying with legal and civic prescriptions, thus reducing the moral or cultural legitimacy of illegal or noncivic actions. This was its message from start to finish. And by sticking to it, Mockus managed not only to implement a set of policy initiatives but also to run a successful communications strategy, which reinforced the former and contributed to achieve its desired results.

But while Mockus's leadership, simultaneously as mayor *and* citizen, did play a fundamental role in the implementation of the civic culture policy, another intervening factor in the effects this initiative had on Bogotá's violence lies in the agentive power of creativity and the arts. Both of them, displayed through symbolism, humor, and subversive language, constitute main components of this initiative. The mayor's leadership and creativity's agency are intimately intertwined. And ultimately the iconoclastic and refreshing character of Mockus's policies can account for his own political success. More than ten years have passed, and most citizens effectively recall civic culture as embodied by pantomime performances at the city's crossroads, by the symbolic power of approval or disapproval of the thumbs-up and thumbs-down cards used by drivers and pedestrians, or the giant carrots displayed as a trademark of the administration. But while the precise effect of these creative and artistic instances is almost impossible to quantify, their agentive power can be theoretically accounted for.

If one of the civic culture policy's main achievements was to restore and enhance communication between the citizenry and the authorities, what was the role that creativity and the arts played in this effort? Here I offer a twofold answer: creativity and the arts lent themselves, on the one hand, as effective tools for giving the concept of temperance a new meaning; and on the other, following Doris Sommer, as estrangement mechanisms that broke "the spell of indifference to rules and refreshed the public's perception of mutual dependence or vulnerability on the streets."[21]

In her ethnographic account of how the Temperance Law came into being, Ángela Rivas Gamboa recalls how, when asked by the local news media about the control of alcohol consumption in the city, Mockus came up with the concept of temperance (*lo zanahorio*) out of the blue.[22] *Zanahorio/a*, in its masculine and feminine forms, literally translates into English as "carrot-like." Traditionally understood in a pejorative sense, this adjective is applied in Colombia, especially among young people, to someone considered dull or boring for exhibiting overly temperate behavior. However, during the Mockus administration, this word underwent a process whereby it was given a radically different meaning. Now the concept of temperance has been vindicated and is associated with a certain way for people to exercise their citizenship. To be *zanahorio/a* is to be able to interact with other citizens, the authorities, and the city in compliance with a set of minimum shared standards for peaceful coexistence; it is, in short, the result of breaching the gap between the legal, moral, and cultural regulatory systems of human behavior.

Mockus as mayor, and hence as a representative of the state, constantly performed the role of a *zanahorio* citizen, whether dressed as a superhero called *Supercitizen* or displaying conducts that would conform to the concept. This fact not only conveyed great credibility to the whole process, but also consolidated Mockus as an agent of change, something that is corroborated in the almost unanimous association between the former mayor and the concept

NEW DIRECTIONS FOR YOUTH DEVELOPMENT • DOI: 10.1002/yd

of civic pedagogy.[23] This function allowed Mockus to closely inter-act with the citizenry and broadly pose the question of citizenship in terms of rights and, especially, responsibilities.

Furthermore, creativity and the arts had the foremost effect of breaking the citizenry's habitual disregard for basic norms of peace-ful coexistence that had been expressed in a wide array of violent attitudes, from aggressive driving to more deadly practices. As Sommer states in a seminal article on the social and political after-math of artistic interventions, "Artful interruptions can unblock procedures mired in habitual abuses or indifference in order to get those practices back on track."[24]

As part of her argument, Sommer rescues from oblivion a fun-damental concept in aesthetic theory: Viktor Shklovsky's estrange-ment. According to the Russian formalist, this is the intrinsic effect of the aesthetic product, as it alters the perceptive automatism through which people tend to experience the world. This is pre-cisely what the civic culture policy achieved, articulated in a pow-erful paradox that signals both failure and success: "The mimes and participants in other civic games produced the immediately refresh-ing effect of estrangement. But by the time their performances failed as art, they had succeeded in effecting a secondary delayed result; a renewed respect for law that brought Bogotá a step closer to coordinating law with culture and morality."[25]

Nevertheless, while I do not challenge Sommer's assessment, it is my contention that between the implementation of creativity and the arts as policy tools and the change in the way citizens interacted with each other, the authorities, and the city as the ultimate effect of this policy lies an intermediate stance: the fact that aesthetic estrangement fundamentally constituted a strategic communicative effort on the part of the administration. Thus understood, and amid a profound distrust of traditional politics, the creative and art-ful elements of the civic culture policy can be accountable for restoring and enhancing communication between the citizenry and the authorities, making citizens realize that there was something wrong in the way they exercised their condition as such. Hence, this renewed respect for the law constitutes a mediated effect of aesthetic estrangement: between the failure of art and the success of policy lies the activation of effective channels of bidirectional communication between the citizenry and the authorities. As traditional grounds of contestation, there can hardly be a better way of doing so than creativity and the arts: "Art can enable politics by interrupting deadlocks, intersecting debates to get past an impasse of breakdown and facilitate a return to procedure."[26]

Conclusion

This article has examined Bogotá's decrease in violence as the result, albeit partial, of the civic culture policy, while at the same time interpreting this policy initiative as a broader philosophical and social project, at the core of which lies the will to redress the way citizenship is perceived and exercised.

The civic culture policy advocates for the emergence of a new type of citizen—a *zanahorio* citizen—as the result of breaching the gap between the legal, moral, and cultural regulatory systems of human behavior. The *zanahorio* citizen is characterized by the awareness not only of his or her rights but also his or her responsibilities, an awareness that leads to self-regulation and compliance with legal and civic provisions. It also advocates for a different way of exercising political power: not through coercion and top-down authority but through direct communication with the citizenry.

In this way, personal leadership and the agentive power of creativity and the arts have played a fundamental role in accomplishing the objectives of this initiative. It is possible that were it not for Mockus's positive example, not only in the face of a water shortage but also constantly performing the role of a *zanahorio* citizen, and for his communication skills and artful interventions, the civic culture policy would not have had the slightest impact on the way citizens interacted with each other, the authorities, and the city.

This interpretation of Bogotá's experience has three important theoretical implications in connection with youth development initiatives. First is the idea that neither citizenship nor the way it is exercised constitute cultural givens; change can be effected and people can in fact interact with one another, the authorities, and the city in more democratic and inclusive ways. Second is the idea that for better or worse, this change can be effected by enhancing communication between the authorities and the citizenry and by broadening the sphere of deliberation. Third, and most important, is the idea that a top-down exercise of political power can be replaced by a pedagogical approach to public administration as an effective model of democratic governance. Let us not forget that Mockus was first and foremost an educator who put himself in charge of a classroom of 6.5 million people. This is a model that could be replicated on a smaller scale in youth development initiatives, where creativity and the arts could be used as tools to reactivate effective channels of communication, implementing a more democratic and bidirectional exercise of authority.

However, when attempting to export Mockus's model to other contexts, a call for caution in the overenthusiastic assessment of this initiative is in order. First and foremost, by looking at Bogotá's historical homicide rate, it is not difficult to see that the major decline presented itself in 1994, a year before Mockus took office. This renders impossible any attempt to establish direct causality between the civic culture policy and the shift in the city's violence trend. Perhaps this shift had to do with the start of an institutional effort during the Jaime Castro administration (1992–1994) to reorganize the city and claim violence control as a local responsibility. Nevertheless, this question remains open and does not undermine the fact that after the initiative was implemented, the tendency continued and even became more pronounced at one point.

Second, caution is called for because of the difficulty of accurately assessing the impact of the civic culture policy on violence in the city. As many scholars acknowledge, this is due to a lack of accurate and comprehensive data, whether about alcohol consumption before and after the implementation of the Temperance Law or about the relationship between the geographical distribution of homicide rates and the geographical origin of the weapons collected during the disarmament campaigns.

NEW DIRECTIONS FOR YOUTH DEVELOPMENT • DOI: 10.1002/yd

This lack of information has led to different assessments and interpretations of this initiative, some more enthusiastic than others. While I do not challenge these assessments—in fact, some of them feed into my argument—one overlooked factor also played a role: the civic culture policy's creative and artful interventions as a means to strengthen communication between the authorities and the citizenry and redress the way citizens perceived and exercised their condition as such.

Ultimately I hope to have conveyed throughout this article the need to think creatively when addressing such complex issues as urban violence. Hard-line options might seem more desirable or effective. Nevertheless, I believe their effects to be limited in their own immediacy. In this sense, Bogotá's experience is a good example of how, even in the most difficult circumstances, creative and communicative pedagogy can be important tools for reducing the level of violence and facilitating peaceful coexistence among citizens.

Notes

1. Acero, H. (2002). Seguridad y convivencia en Bogotá: Logros y retos 1995–2001. In F. Carrión (Ed.), *Seguridad ciudadana, ¿espejismo o realidad?* Quito: FLACSO.

2. Acero. (2002).

3. Acero, H. (2005). La seguridad ciudadana una responsabilidad de los gobiernos locales en Colombia. In L. Dammert & G. Paulsen (Eds.), *Ciudad y seguridad en América Latina*. Santiago de Chile: FLACSO; Llorente, M. V., & Rivas, A. (2004). La caída del crimen en Bogotá: Una década de políticas de seguridad ciudadana. In L. Dammert (Ed.), *Seguridad ciudadana: Experiencias y desafíos*. Valparaiso: Ilustre Municipalidad de Valparaiso.

4. In a longer version of this article, I also argue that the institutional context under which the civic culture policy was implemented is also one of the factors that can help account for its impact.

5. Mockus, A. (2002). *Cultura ciudadana, programa contra la violencia en Santa Fe de Bogotá, Colombia, 1995–1997*. Washington, DC: Inter-American Development Bank. P. 7 (My translation).

6. Llorente & Rivas. (2004).

7. Mockus. (2002).

8. After the implementation of the Temperance Law, and between 1996 and 1998, the number of homicides dropped from 3,303 to 2,482, and the number of deaths in traffic accidents from 1,301 to 914. Acero. (2002).

9. Mockus. (2002).

10. Llorente & Rivas. (2004).

11. Mockus. (2002).

12. Mockus. (2002).

13. Mockus. (2002).

14. Llorente & Rivas. (2004).

15. Mockus. (2002).

16. Mockus. (2002).

17. Acero. (2002); Concha-Eastman, A. (2002). Urban violence in Latin America and the Caribbean: Dimensions, explanations, actions. In S. Rotker (Ed.), *Citizens of fear: Urban violence in Latin America*. New Brunswick, NJ: Rutgers University Press; Mockus. (2002).

18. Llorente, M. V., Nuñez, J., and & Rubio, M. (1999). *Efectos de los controles al consumo de alcohol y al porte de armas de fuego en la violencia homicida.* Retrieved May 5, 2008, from http://www.suivd.gov.co/investigaciones/Alcohol%20&%20Armas.htm.

19. It is worth noting that the figures that are often cited by scholars are the ones pertaining to the city's homicide rate between 1993 and 2002, in which time it registered a plunge from 80 to 28 homicides per 100,000 people. However, here I chose to present the figures just for the period between 1995 and 1999, so they would coincide with the initial implementation of the Temperance Law and the time when the econometric analysis was produced. Acero. (2002).

20. Rojas, C. (2005). Descentralización y la cultura ciudadana de Bogotá, Colombia. In I. Licha (Ed.), *Ciudadanía activa: Gestión de presupuestos locales en Asia Oriental y América Latina*. Washington, DC: Inter-American Development Bank.

21. Sommer, D. (2005). Art and accountability. *Review: Literature and arts of the Americas, 38*(1), 261–276. P. 269.

22. Rivas Gamboa, A. (2007). *Gorgeous monster: The arts of governing and managing violence in Bogotá*. Saarbrucken: VDM Verlag Dr. Muller. P. 70.

23. Pizano, L. (2003). *Bogotá y el cambio: Percepciones sobre la ciudad y la ciudadanía*. Bogotá: Universidad Nacional de Colombia.

24. Sommer. (2005). P. 269.

25. Sommer. (2005). P. 269.

26. Sommer. (2005). P. 269.

FELIPE CALA BUENDÍA *is a doctoral student in the Department of Spanish and Portuguese Languages and Cultures at Princeton University.*

NEW DIRECTIONS FOR YOUTH DEVELOPMENT • DOI: 10.1002/yd

Indigenous cultures develop radio programming to maintain home languages, gain access to education, greet friends and relatives, and re-create traditional culture under circumstances of modern pressures and opportunities. The authors explore these contributions to voicing cultural diversity in the global era.

2

Voicing differences: Indigenous and urban radio in Argentina, Chile, and Nigeria

Luis E. Cárcamo-Huechante,
Nicole Delia Legnani

HOW CAN RADIO FOSTER the continuity of indigenous languages and oral traditions, especially among the younger generations who have lost their connection to them? Is there an aesthetic of linguistic, ethnic, and cultural difference voiced and performed through intercultural initiatives in radio communications? How do local and indigenous community radio programs foster the creativity of young people, as well as their connection to community traditions? In the face of these challenges and questions, the endeavors of indigenous and local radio producers and broadcasters offer creative ways to revitalize a sense of community and cultural memory, as well as contribute to a more diverse audio public sphere in society.

NEW DIRECTIONS FOR YOUTH DEVELOPMENT, NO. 125, SPRING 2010 © WILEY PERIODICALS, INC.
Published online in Wiley InterScience (www.interscience.wiley.com) • DOI: 10.1002/yd.336

In this article, we highlight the ways in which Mapuche radio programs in South America, as well as similar creative uses of radio in Nigeria, have enabled local communities to voice their cultural differences and establish material and symbolic connections among people, with a stellar role for young activists. In these experiences, indigenous and local radio producers and broadcasters have developed imaginative strategies for using radio in a context of people's dispersion and displacement, thus building their own acoustic and sonorous space as minority subjects amid the hegemonic noise of mainstream media.

Mapping Mapurbe radio

Mapurbe is an ingenious and indigenous neologism. It was playfully coined by Santiago-based Mapuche poet David Añiñir to name a new indigenous identity, that of Mapuches, who now live in Argentine and Chilean cities.[1] As a composite term, *Mapurbe* is the result of a fusion between two words: *Mapu*, which means land, earth, country, or universe in Mapudungun (the Mapuche language), and *urbe*, which means city in Spanish. This neologism constitutes an ingenious bilingual way of naming a new urban landscape that has been reshaped by the recent waves of Mapuche migration from rural areas to major urban centers; a process through which Mapuche communities appropriate and redefine the symbolic and spatial configuration of cities. Subsequently, this bilingual figure has also become the way in which urban Mapuches identify themselves.

Under this distinctive identity, the Equipo de Comunicación Mapurbe in southern Argentina is one among many experiences that involve members of the new generations of Mapuches who have grown up in cities and who know how to play the game of modern media and know how to carry out a cross-cultural use of radio. Through radio airwaves and community networks, young indigenous and nonindigenous people have created ways to reimagine their urban spaces. This background is what two members of the Equipo de Comunicación Mapurbe, Lorena Cañuqueo and Laura Kropff, highlight:

The members who make up the Mapurbe Communication team [including the authors of this article] are mostly young Mapuches who live on the outskirts of Bariloche. Many members participated in community FM radios during the latter part of the 1990s. This period was defined by the country's application of neoliberal policies, which led to an increase in unemployment and across-the-board budget cuts for government agencies. Youth participation in the outer neighborhoods was framed, in some cases, by the student movement, which defended public education, and in others by social protests that responded to unemployment and precarious labor conditions. Also, a parallel performance circuit known as *under* emerged in these neighborhoods and was connected to different social movements. This circuit called itself heavy-punk resistance [our translation].[2]

As part of these social, political, and cultural networks, the members of the Equipo Mapurbe in 2002 developed a series of initiatives under the name Campaña de Autoafirmación Mapuche. The campaign focused on the Mapuches living in urban areas and young people in particular, including those already involved in the heavy punk resistance circuit. This project aimed to develop a sense of community, memory, and identity among the members of the dispersed Mapuche community of southern Argentina, specifically within the provinces of Río Negro and Neuquén. Moreover, this cultural activism has constantly been linked back to the more political and economic struggle for their land rights, which is a way for Mapurbes to relate with Mapuches living in rural areas.

In Argentina, the Encuesta Complementaria de Pueblos Indígenas, a survey carried out in 2004–2005 by the Argentine State, verified the existence of 105,000 people of indigenous origin, of whom over 70 percent live in the provinces of Chubut, Neuquén, and Río Negro.[3] One of the major criticisms about this survey in Argentina was that it underestimated and practically dismissed the existence of Mapuches in urban areas. Yet the urban Mapuches have made their presence known by identifying themselves as Mapurbes, thus calling attention to their underrecognized demographic.

"Micro" economics and aesthetics

Under these particular circumstances of relocation and misrepresentation, how can urban Mapuches maintain and renew their traditions? This concern has guided the founders of the Equipo de Comunicación Mapurbe as they develop radio communications projects in conjunction with aesthetic and cultural forms of public action in southern Argentina. The Equipo de Comunicación Mapurbe has worked primarily in three areas: theater workshops, a printed publication titled *Mapurbes*, and radio programs. A key aspect of their initiatives in these areas has been to delve into communication: into the Mapurbes' language, style of speaking, and manner of voicing their selves.

At the same time, as a result of their precarious financial resources and, thus, limited access to infrastructure and technology, the Equipo has conceptualized the idea of the *micros*, which are a series of three- to five-minute radio programs. Indeed, the creative economics of the *micros* is what has allowed the Equipo de Comunicación Mapurbe to rent airtime from different radio stations with a very low budget. To produce these radio programs, the team mostly depends on contributions from each member's regional Mapuche community. Their experience shows that radio is flexible, adaptable, and affordable. Indeed, this flexibility of radio economics has made it the medium most frequently employed by indigenous communities and activists in Latin America.

Another striking feature of the *micros* is that it allows Mapurbe broadcasters to stake out more territory on the radio dial, despite, or perhaps because of, their limited time slots. The *micros* creatively compress different aspects of their community's culture into a few minutes of airtime. Often the *micros* juxtapose and mix ancestral legends, family narratives, personal and collective stories, music, and political platforms. For example, one of their *micro* programs starts by invoking a traditional Mapuche legend: that of the *kai kai* serpent. Then a community activist speaks about issues of discrimination and land conflicts. Meanwhile, in the background, we hear sounds of traditional musical instruments, mainly *kultrun*. Finally,

NEW DIRECTIONS FOR YOUTH DEVELOPMENT • DOI: 10.1002/yd

the summons of "natural beings" and the closing insertion of a speech in Mapudungun refers back to the ancestral legend of the *kai kai*. In this way, instead of a single narrative-oriented script, the Equipo de Comunicación Mapurbe opts for a polyphonic assemblage of voices and multiple narratives. Their manner of speaking through radio includes multiple voices; in this way, the *micros* represent a polyphonic way of broadcasting.

Mapudungun: Of the earth and on the air!

On the other side of the Andes, in Chile, Mapuche activists also seek to build their own public spaces in the cities, especially through radio. *Wixage Anai!* (Wake up, get up!) is the name of one of the most innovative Mapuche radio programs in a country whose overall population is over 15 million people, and 600,000 are Mapuches.[4] Based in Santiago, the Chilean capital city, *Wixage anai!* has been on the air since 1993 and has been broadcast in two languages: Spanish and Mapudungun. This bilingual radio program was initially led by Ramón Curivil, a high school teacher and intercultural educator. Other key members of the team are Elías Paillán, now the main leader of the group; Elizabeth Huenchual; and José Paillal. All of them are strongly committed to political and cultural activism and are fully bilingual in Spanish and Mapudungun.

In the early 1990s, the program obtained some nongovernmental funding to be hosted on Radio Nacional de Chile, the state-owned radio station with the widest reach in Chile, from Arica to Patagonia, and beyond. By the mid-1990s, however, the Mapuche radio program was unable to obtain further funding from sponsors and had to start fundraising within the community. *Wixage Anai!* is currently broadcast from Radio Tierra, a station that emerged under the umbrella of the major nongovernmental center for women in Santiago, Casa de la Mujer La Morada, founded by feminist activists and independent scholars in the 1980s. It airs on Radio Tierra from 7:00 to 8:00 P.M. on Mondays, Wednesdays, and Saturdays.

NEW DIRECTIONS FOR YOUTH DEVELOPMENT • DOI: 10.1002/yd

Elías Paillán, one of the key members in the initial stages of this radio program, describes the principal design of their initiative in the following terms:

Wixage Anai's main objectives were, from its very inception on that cold winter day on June 26, 1993, to animate Mapuche life in the countryside and in the city, that is, to promote Mapundungun speech, Mapuche socio-cultural practices, religion, and sports in order to keep [our] culture alive. On the one hand, in the city, due to the increase in the Mapuche population that migrated to urban centers in search of a better life; and, on the other hand, in the countryside, to serve those who remain on the land and who, many times, are alone. Another objective was to build a bridge of human relationships between Mapuche families in the city and in the countryside as a response to migration by reconnecting people through broadcasting, sending messages and uniting them in spite of the distance [our translation].

With these words, Paillán highlights the cultural role as well as the communicative importance of *Wixage anai!* for a Mapuche people subject to weakening community ties due to migration. According to a study conducted by the Centro de Estudios Públicos in July 2002, poverty affects many Mapuche families living in rural areas.[5] This reality, along with the urban promise of new opportunities, beckons young Mapuches to major cities in Chile, such as Santiago, Concepción, and Temuco. Indeed, recent data show that 124,459 Mapuches live in Greater Santiago, particularly in under-served and populous areas such as Peñalolén, Cerro Navia, El Bosque, and San Bernardo.

The fact that *Wixage Anai!* is aired in Santiago, with strong ties to this urban Mapuche population and especially the new Mapurbe generation, situates it within a community-building process that is struggling against the loss of linguistic and cultural memory among *Mapurbes*. As Paillán suggests, the Mapuche program has gone further by developing a creative way to reach the more traditional Mapuche communities of the Araucanía, a region in southern Chile. Each program is recorded and sent out to the Wallon Radio Station, a Mapuche station based in Likan Ray, a town in the heart of Araucanía. Through this process, *Wixage Anai!* connects

Mapuche communities and individuals within a sprawling city like Santiago, and also across regions and urban and rural boundaries in times of displacement and dispersion.

Radial reflections: Youth, sports, and elders

Radio programs allow many young urban Mapuches who seek to sustain their indigenous cultural identity to live "on the same frequency" culturally, even in Westernized urban settings such as Santiago. Paillán explicitly comments on the protagonism of the new generation of Mapuches in this process and the way in which they find an identity-based connection through the radio program:

Youth have taken the lead as active collaborators in our radio broadcasting initiatives. They have found in [radio] an important place to reunite with their identity, which often is hidden in their own homes or weakened as a product of the complexities of Western life. *Wixage Anai!*'s radio initiative was worked on and maintained by youth who have raised awareness in others and have thus produced a self-identification in themselves, precisely because these young people have appreciated the value of projecting themselves and feeling proud of their own particular culture. With the program, some young members have created different groups for art, musical, and theatrical productions, teams for the *palin* [a team game]; and advocacy events, such as social and political protests, land rights issues, and more [our translation].

As Paillán contends, the radio program and its cultural initiatives constitute "an important place to reconnect with their identity." For the *Wixage Anai!* team, radio has become an opportunity to create a wide forum for community action, including music, theater, sports, organizational events, and political mobilization. Within this process, arts and politics, recreation and social engagement, pleasure and activism interconnect to foster communication and connection among young Mapurbes.

One of the activities successfully promoted and organized by *Wixage Anai!* is *palin*. *Palin*, also called *chueca* in criollo Chilean discourse, is a Mapuche game in which two teams use wooden sticks to carry a wooden ball to the opposite goals at the ends of a rectangular field, one for each team. The team that puts the ball over the line scores a point. It is played by men, but the actual event incorporates all members of the community, across ages and genders, through prayers, dances, music, cookouts, murals, indigenous rights campaigns, and promotion of the radio program. In the past, all Mapuche communities had their own *palin* teams as well as their own fields.[6]

The Jvken Mapu Center is the broader organization within which the *Wixage Anai!* radio team organizes this type of social and ritual gathering in the Quinta Normal Park on the west side of Santiago, mostly on Sunday or on Mapuche holidays. *Palin* has become one of the most popular activities for young people. It brings them together not only as players but also within their circles of friends, who then use the opportunity to join the different initiatives of *Wixage Anai!* and the Jvken Mapu Center. This is an extraordinary example of how to practice a local and indigenous tradition by using a mixed set of social activities ranging from political activism to games.

Another way in which the program sensitizes its young indigenous and nonindigenous audience toward Mapuche traditions is the incorporation of *testimonios* by the elderly members of the community. Over the years, *Wixage Anai!* has interviewed several Mapuche elders living in Santiago, using this as an opportunity to bring back a specific Mapuche oral tradition: the *nvxam*. According to Ramón Curivil, a Mapuche researcher and founder of this radio program, *nvxam* means "dialogue" or "conversation." In terms of Mapuche tradition, it is a conversation that can include a variety of expository techniques: *epeu* (storytelling), *vlkantun* (singing), *koyaqtun* (collective deliberation; assembly), and *pentukun* (friendly and affectionate talk). By implementing this tradition of speaking, the Mapuche radio program is able to incorporate a mixture of spoken speech and singing within what is conventionally understood as an interview.

Thus, *Wixage Anai!* as a radio program fosters activities that connect its audience, especially young Mapuches, to the cultural richness of their indigenous traditions. We should recall here that the very name of this program, *Wixage Anai!* is a call to the contemporary Mapuche community for a cultural awakening: "Wake up! Get up!" In a similar fashion, the *micros* of the Equipo de Comunicación Mapurbe in southern Argentina perform this task of memory making and cultural revitalization. Within a contemporary context of land struggles, migration, and dispersion for Mapuches in Argentina and Chile, these radio programs not only set Mapuche voices and sounds on the air but also constitute a broader space for connection among young and old generations of the Mapuche nation.

Radio edutainment in Nigeria

Radio voices embody the possibility of symbolic connectedness for many communities. As American radio scholar Michele Hilmes states, "Radio waves and their impervious mobility across social boundaries" have served "as an ideal symbol for national togetherness."[7] In Nigeria, the African Radio Drama Association (ARDA) has written and produced radio programs since 1995 as a way to empower the country's underserved citizens. ARDA-Nigeria's "edutainment for development" projects receive funding from various international sources.[8] Its serial dramas address salient issues such as climate change (*When the Drumbeat Changes You Must Change Your Dance Steps*), sustainable land use (*The Long Dry Season*), and the spread of AIDS among youth (*When the Breeze Blows*) on the air while advancing positive knowledge, attitudes, and practice in community and national development through sponsored activities.

According to Julian Orupabo (personal communication, July 1, 2009), a research and development adviser at ARDA, youth are involved during all production stages of radio projects when this demographic forms part of the target audience.[9] The young population of rural and urban communities is often the focus of ARDA projects, especially in areas such as maternal health and child care and HIV/AIDS prevention and treatment. For these projects,

NEW DIRECTIONS FOR YOUTH DEVELOPMENT • DOI: 10.1002/yd

youth make up 42 percent of all individuals working on the design and analysis, implementation and monitoring, and evaluation and planning stages for radio dramas. The voices of youth are also heard on the air, representing child and teenage characters. In *Omo Catch Up*, ARDA involved street youth in a radio variety show that also informed the public about sexually transmitted infections and promoted sexual responsibility among participants and listeners.

Active participation of the target audience during all stages of production and postproduction (testing, monitoring, and evaluation) gives local community members a stake in the radio program's success. During the airing of the first thirteen episodes and after the final thirteen episodes are aired, young people, other relevant groups, and opinion leaders provide ARDA with necessary feedback. Since the radio dramas combine entertainment and advocacy, ARDA must first understand the knowledge base and practices of target audience members. This is gauged initially through in-depth interviews and focus group discussions. Currently listeners who tune in to ARDA's latest serial drama on best farming practices in the context of climate change (*When the Drumbeat Changes You Must Change Your Dance Steps*) are encouraged to provide feedback by text messaging, phone, mail, e-mail and listening or farmer groups (http://ardaradio.org/climate_change_project). Target audience members recruited during the planning stages of the program often serve as moderators of the listening groups sponsored by ARDA in the community.

Passive audience or active listeners?

The popularity of listening groups is a measure of an ARDA radio program's success. Members of ARDA's listening public meet in groups within their local community to discuss their favorite radio programs. A nationally broadcast radio serial such as *Rainbow City* is expected to reach 30 percent of its target audience (Julian Orupabo, personal communication, August 4, 2009). Radio presenters at local stations estimate the demographic spread of the listening public from the feedback they receive in messages and calls from individual listeners, as well as representatives of listening clubs, community-based organizations, and youth-serving organizations. Yet ARDA does not measure its success solely on the popularity of its shows; it also considers changes in knowledge, attitude, and practice among members of the target audience. By promoting various venues for dialogue among community members, ARDA emphasizes active listening, that is, critical thought, discussion, and engagement with the story and the underlying issues.

Paulo Freire's *Pedagogy of the Oppressed* inspired ARDA's creative directors to promote local forums in familiar spaces where radio audiences may engage in active listening and involve themselves in the conflicts and resolutions broadcast on the air.[10] A fictional plot, often a love story that inspires the passions of its audience members while representing their conditions and aspirations in their own languages and sociocultural contexts, is often the catalyst for productive discussions by community members. Adegbe Martins notes that thinking critically about characters—their motivations and actions—and their fictional lives as they are affected by contemporary issues, reinforces a sense of community as listening group members find common ground through communication.[11] ARDA also distributes tape recorders and cassettes of the latest episodes so that members may listen to missed episodes or review past episodes in greater detail. (The tapes are especially important in areas where signal quality or reception is poor.) Listening clubs also use the tape players to record their own sessions, thus providing ARDA with valuable feedback. Members answer quizzes and calls to action, and they enter contests. By focusing on community members' involvement in the radio drama's reception as well its production, a fictional plot becomes a creative vehicle for cross-community debate and empowerment.

Voicing diversity and difference

Nigeria's cultural and ethnic diversity require local community involvement and leadership for the stories and messages produced by ARDA to remain authentic. ARDA's programming in rural areas serves Nigerian citizens by broadcasting in each region's indigenous languages (for example, Housa in northern Nigeria and

Yorubá in southern Nigeria). Creating a program that represents the cultural and linguistic diversity of urban settings has proved challenging. To date, ARDA's most successful program is the radio drama *Rainbow City*, which gained an important following in rural and urban sectors alike.[12]

Rainbow City's creative directors hoped to convey cultural and class distinctions of Nigerian society without resorting to stereotypes in a radio drama that touched on a variety of common concerns arising from urban poverty: police brutality, government accountability, exploitation by local elites, inheritance conflicts, family life, and sexual or reproductive health. *Rainbow City* also promoted democratic ideals and practices before, during, and after Nigeria's transition to civilian government in 1999. Since ARDA's ambitions with *Rainbow City* were projected on a national level, the radio drama was written in a multi-inflected English script that sought to reflect the diversity of Nigeria's cities such as Lagos or the capital, Abuja.[13] The dialogues, which are at times in pidgin English, are infused with proverbs, riddles, and jokes to engage the listening public with a language that is both familiar and involved, thus facilitating understanding while encouraging critical thought (Julian Orupabo, personal communication, August 4, 2009).

ARDA's sensitivity to regional and national idioms is reflected in the attention its producers give to music in each radio drama. The music and sounds of the region being served bridge scenes within episodes. The signature tune is an important aspect of each radio drama and is composed to represent both the story and local music traditions. In places where local stations broadcast ARDA serial productions, it is quite common to hear people humming and singing these signature tunes in doorways and on streets and, in doing so, they recognize one another as citizens of the same listening public, involved in the same fictional lives which speak in so many ways to their own.

Tasks for all of us

The indigenous airwaves create an audible reference point whereby local communities of the Mapuche people keep alive their linguistic, cultural, and social togetherness. No doubt these radio initiatives perform a key role in the Latin American context at large where all indigenous peoples face the issue of continued dispersion. The ARDA-Nigeria experience also offers a compelling trial in radio programming to be re-created in other communities and countries. For example, Spanish-speaking audiences are already familiar with the format of *telenovela* (soap opera), an influential audiovisual discourse in Latin American popular culture. This television genre has a particular equivalent in the tradition of Latin American radio communications: that of *radioteatro* or *radionovela*, known as radio drama (sometimes linked to audio drama or audio theater) in the English-speaking world. Writing and broadcasting radio dramas can open spaces to voice the issues of marginalized groups within a fictional plot, and it can broaden their public appeal by virtue of storytelling's excitement of the senses.

Doris Sommer has demonstrated that love stories engaged newly formed Latin American republics in the nineteenth century and were creative tools for imagining nations.[14] If at that time these narratives constituted the fictions of the *criollo* agents of Latin American nations with the novel as their medium, now the task could be to create indigenous foundational fictions through radio. With the cultural agency of indigenous radio producers and broadcasters, this type of communicative aesthetic—that of *radioteatro* or radio drama—may renew indigenous radio programming, and it may allow them to expand and widen their local and regional audiences.

Why is it important to support the struggle of these local voices and narratives for a wider audience in contemporary society? How do these radio projects teach us to address not only the expectations of local communities but also the hopes of generations who are growing up in the contemporary audio culture of radio, television, cell phones, MP3, and others? For urban and nonurban young people alike, being in touch with community traditions through sounds and voices, which emerge on the airwaves, makes a difference. The creative use of radio renders the younger generations sensitive to the educational and cultural value of pluralism on the very level of the senses: listening to and experiencing a more diverse audio environment. As we have seen in the case of *Rainbow City*, ARDA responded to this challenge by creating a polytonal and multi-inflected script in English, the hegemonic language of Nigeria. Likewise, one of the great success stories of the *micros* and *Wixage Anai!* in Argentina and Chile, respectively, has been the revival of the Mapuche people's language for younger generations through bilingual broadcasts in Spanish and Mapudungun from urban settlements.

Indigenous and community radio stations and programs in the Americas and across the globe are making linguistic and cultural differences audible, thus contributing to the struggle for a more diverse audio public sphere in contemporary society. In addition, they enable local communities to build and develop their own symbolic and material spaces in increasingly complex media systems and allow young people to connect with local languages and cultures. Radio thus becomes an art of communication and an art of community.

Notes

1. See Añiñir, D. (2005). *Mapurbe*. Santiago, Chile: Autoedition.

2. Cañuqueo, L., and Kropff, L. (2005). Reflexiones sobre el trabajo del Equipo de Comunicación Mapurbe. *Seminario Anual "Performance y raíces"* 5. Hemispheric Institute of Performance and Politics at NYU and Universidad Federal de Minas Gerais. http://hemi.nyu.edu/bb/phpBB2/download.php?id=183.

3. Instituto Nacional de Estadísticas y Censos. (2006). *ECPI: Encuesta Complementaria de Pueblos Indígenas.* Buenos Aires: República de Argentina, Ministerio de Economía, Secretaría de Programación Económica y Regional, Instituto Nacional de Estadística y Censos.

4. Instituto de Estudios Indígenas. (2003). *Los derechos de los pueblos indígenas en Chile: informe del programa de derechos indígenas.* Santiago, Chile: LOM Ediciones/Universidad de la Frontera.

5. Centro de Estudios Públicos. (2002). *Estudio Nacional de Opinión Pública #5. Tercera Serie: Julio 2002. Tema Especial: Una Radiografía de los Mapuches.* Santiago, Chile: Documento de Trabajo #345.

6. This ancient Mapuche game has been compared to hockey by Western scholars and writers because of their similarities. See http://www.beingindigenous.org/magazine/palin.htm.

7. Hilmes, M. (2002). *Radio reader. Essays in the cultural history of radio.* New York: Routledge. P. xi.

8. These include the United States Information Service, Ford Foundation, International Development Research Center, Farm Radio International, Women Farmers Action Network, University of Guelph, and Shell.

9. The National Population Commission estimates the current population of Nigeria to be about 126 million. National Population Commission [Nigeria] and ORC Macro. (2004). *Nigeria Demographic and Health Survey 2003.* Calverton, MD: National Population Commission and ORC Macro. Twenty-three percent of all Nigerians are between ten and eighteen years of age and 22 percent of all Nigerian youth will bear children during their adolescent years. Federal Office of Statistics [Nigeria] and IRD/ Macro International. (2000). Nigeria Demographic and Health Survey, 1999. Lagos, Nigeria: Federal Office of Statistics: Columbia, Md.; IRD/Macro International.

10. Freire, P. (c. 1970). *Pedagogy of the oppressed* (M. B. Ramos, Trans.). New York: Herder and Herder.

11. Adegbc Martins, A. (2003). Radio drama for development: ARDA and the *Rainbow City* experience. *Journal of African Cultural Studies, 16*(1), 95–105.

12. The success of this serial drama, ARDA's longest-running radio program to date, also served as a capacity-building project for over twenty-five radio stations in Nigeria.

13. Nigeria's population is primarily rural. Only one-third of Nigerians live in urban sectors of the country. National Population Commission [Nigeria] and ORC Macro. (2004). *Nigeria Demographic and Health Survey 2003.* Calverton, Md.: National Population Commission and ORC Macro.

14. Sommer, D. (1991). *Foundational fictions: The national romances of Latin America.* Berkeley: University of California Press.

LUIS E. CÁRCAMO-HUECHANTE *teaches Latin American and Indigenous literatures and cultures at the University of Texas at Austin.*

NICOLE DELIA LEGNANI *is a doctoral student in Spanish and Latin American literatures at Harvard University.*

In countries with precarious cultural infrastructures, initiatives based on arts education can play a significant role in the transformation and civic development of youth.

3

Silent gains: Instituto Buena Bista and art as catalyst among Curaçaoan youth

Iberia Pérez González

SINCE ITS INCEPTION IN SEPTEMBER 2006, the Instituto Buena Bista (IBB), a center for contemporary art in the Dutch Caribbean island of Curaçao, has been strongly committed to promoting the value of the visual arts and providing a place where Curaçaoan youth can develop their imagination and creative skills. The three-month research internship I conducted in this institute between October 2007 and January 2008, based primarily on interviews with key sources and art historical and archival research, demonstrated that initiatives based on arts education can act as a catalyst in the formation of social agents not only by fostering an alternative approach to education through visual arts training but, most important, stimulating new forms of citizenship. In this article, I discuss how this contemporary art center is engaged with shaping the character, perspectives, and values of the Curaçaoan community by instilling youth with a *buena bista*—a positive and renewed view of themselves, their future, and their island.[1]

WILEY
InterScience®
DISCOVER SOMETHING GREAT

NEW DIRECTIONS FOR YOUTH DEVELOPMENT, NO. 125, SPRING 2010 © WILEY PERIODICALS, INC.
Published online in Wiley InterScience (www.interscience.wiley.com) • DOI: 10.1002/yd.337

Filling the void

In order to understand the importance of such an organization, it is necessary to start by framing it within some general but vital observations regarding its context. As Dutch historian Gert Oostindie has noted, the island of Curaçao has been undergoing an economic and social crisis due to growing economic disparities, strong social and racial segregation, low-level education and poor educational performance, high levels of unemployment, and high crime rates and violence, especially among youth.[2] This crisis has been interpreted by researchers, as Oostindie has noted, as evidence "not only of failing governance on Curaçao but also of dysfunctionality of Curaçaoan culture as such."[3]

As my research revealed, the poor conditions regarding resources for the arts and the absence of a strong cultural infrastructure in Curaçao can be explained to a great extent by the scant attention the local government has paid over the years to developing the visual arts and other cultural affairs. According to Gibi Bacilio, a policymaker in the Ministry of Culture and Education of Curaçao, the government's primary concerns have been mainly directed toward reinforcing its economic industry and more basic social issues of housing, public health, and education. As a consequence, the arts and culture have been disregarded.[4] This has led to a noticeable cultural illiteracy that is closely linked to the poor educational system and particularly to the scarcity of resources pertaining to arts education on the island. At the university level, study programs do not encourage the development of creative skills but focus primarily on disciplines that can ensure young Curaçaoans access to the labor market.

This state of affairs set some of the primary conditions for the emergence of the IBB in Curaçao. Yet its conceptualization as a long-term proposition followed as a logical consequence of community-based arts projects promoted by the ArteSwa Foundation. This organization was created in 2004 by Dutch artist David Bade, along with his brother Herman Bade and art historian Jennifer Smit in Curaçao.[5] *Swa* is a word in Papiamento that refers to fraternization or brotherhood. Thus, as the name suggests, through ArteSwa workshops, the creators seek to engage a wide range of members from society, including school children from all levels, with the intention of erasing social boundaries and stimulating creative situations that can connect people who would not normally interact. As an outcome of these workshops, ArteSwa members realized that there was no professional framework for the development of young talent among the islanders. It was clear that if the visual arts and the local culture were to be strengthened, a new space would be needed to support it. With this in mind, artists David Bade and Tirzo Martha, along with art historian Nancy Hoffmann, founded the IBB in April 2006.

The establishment of this nonprofit organization aimed at filling the cultural void by providing a platform for the development of local visual arts and to advocate for the importance of arts and culture in Curaçaoan society by focusing on the education of young talent. To comply with these objectives the IBB structured a well-rounded program based on three interrelated components: (1) an educational program where talented youngsters receive an intensive but basic art education for a minimum period of one year; (2) an international space program, where an artist or curator from abroad is invited to do workshops, lectures, or interventions in the public space; and (3) a national artist-in-residence program, where a Dutch artist is invited for a three-month period to reside and work at the institute.

Since both the international and national residence programs are conditioned by a direct and close collaboration between the visiting artists and the IBB students, their interaction plays an important role in the students' formation. In addition to these collaborations, the students participate in a variety of intensive two-week seminars on different art techniques: drawing, painting, three-dimensional structures, multimedia, video art, and the like. The goals of these practical courses are for the students to learn how to work with different materials, surfaces, and formats and also to learn basic art principles like observation, originality, and critical awareness. The lack of referents in the immediate surroundings accounts for the intensity of the seminar courses given by Bade and Martha, as well as some of the visiting artists.

Alongside the hands-on training, the creative formation of the IBB students is complemented with basic art history courses. These courses, focused on local and Caribbean art as well as Western art history, aim at fostering the students' critical thought processes and a better understanding of more conceptual principles of art making and the history of art.

The educational program at the IBB is directed to young Antilleans ranging primarily between the ages of fifteen and twenty-five. The scouting of these talented youngsters usually takes place through their participation in the ArteSwa community arts projects, referral of their teachers, or through their assistance on the open house celebrated at the IBB at the end of each semester. Every year, over thirty students apply to the IBB program, and approximately fifteen are selected. During the selection process, the applicants participate in a personal interview where they are evaluated according to their motivation and enthusiasm to engage in arts education and on the quality of a drawing sample or other artwork done by the student.

At the end of the program, the students are evaluated on their performance and progress and are given the opportunity to show their work to the local community at an art exhibition held on the IBB premises.

This course is mainly an after-school program and does not lead to an academic degree or diploma. However, the IBB's educational curriculum is intended to function as a springboard to more advanced art schools, and so its leading members are strongly committed to encouraging, guiding, and assisting talented students so they can continue their formal arts training abroad.

Trial and error

Not too long ago, having artistic ambitions had been simply unthinkable for Dutch Antilleans. This can be explained due to the limited opportunities for creative education available on the island, the meager art market, and the scarce job opportunities for artists within the cultural industry. Furthermore, the fact that the visual arts have long been considered an elitist endeavor exclusive to the upper classes and in no way regarded as a profession has played a crucial role in the underdevelopment of the Curaçaoan art scene. Notwithstanding, in a recent interview, artist-mentor Tirzo Martha made a remark about a Curaçaoan girl who said, "My dream will come true thanks to the IBB." It would seem that traditionally held (mis)conceptions about the potential and value of the visual arts are changing. The opportunity to engage in aesthetic experiences at the IBB is allowing Curaçaoan youth to look at their lives in a newly meaningful way, increasing their likelihood of setting further educational goals and aiming at other than practical fields as a career option.

Interestingly, IBB's overall approach and pedagogical methods are much more untraditional, open, and flexible than a regular art school. Hence, I believe much of the success of this organization relies on the fact that the learning process occurs through informal though solid structures of education and taking as a point of departure the individual circumstances of each student within the informal context of everyday life. Because the age and maturity levels of the students vary, the IBB strongly emphasizes the value of small classes, limiting their admissions to approximately twelve to fifteen students per academic year, as David Bade explained in an interview. Although every student participates in the same program, focusing on small groups enables artist-mentors to provide more personal coaching, paying attention to the individual needs of each student in terms of age, maturity, language limitations, and artistic level.

The exchange between the national and international artists in residence and the students is of utmost importance and contributes to the strength and the uniqueness of the IBB's curriculum. The opportunity to become acquainted with different practices, materials, and points of view through regular and dynamic interaction with artists from abroad allows IBB students not only to gain a new understanding of the potential of different mediums and the multiple possibilities of art but also to expand their limits outside the confines of the island. In my perspective, this intercultural interaction greatly contributes to the cultural competence of the students and facilitates greater awareness of their cultural identity based on values like openness and diversity.

Since many of the students enrolled at the IBB come from disadvantaged social and economic backgrounds, artist-mentors emphasize fostering a strong sense of community and equality among the group. Moreover, they are constantly looking for new ways of mediating information in order to hold the students' attention and keep them focused on their artistic goals. Effective communication is reached by forgoing hierarchical positions and avoiding highly coded expressions or excessively formal speech, a situation that heightens the students' self-assurance and makes them feel more comfortable at the school.

It could be argued that IBB's pedagogical philosophy is based on principles of autonomy and confidence, essential elements of creativity and innovation. Because the artist-mentors have great confidence in the students, rules and regulations tend to be few, allowing flexibility for the free flow of imagination and providing enough space so the students can feel comfortable to be themselves: young, curious, and playful.

In only two years of operation, the arts-based IBB program has exceeded the expectations of many: Some of the students have been selected to participate in visual art contests, and approximately fifteen of them have been granted scholarships for continuing their formal training, mainly in Dutch art academies. Nevertheless, as the IBB continues its process of trial-and-error searching for the best ways to structure the organization to meet their own expectations as well as the needs of the students, they continue to face challenges and limitations that sometimes hinder their efforts, as well as the educational and social projections of the initiative.

According to my research, one of the most pressing challenges for the IBB is the limited reception they have within the local community. In general, the Curaçaoan people seem to be quite resistant in supporting and embracing efforts that do not explicitly refer to their own traditions—mainly the values and traditions that correspond to their African heritage. Moreover, since the visual arts are regarded by most of the population as "an area of culture that has been monopolized by the elite groups," according to Rene Rosalia, director of Kas di Kultura, a center for contemporary art like the IBB could sometimes seem at odds with a public that does not feel that art and its institutions share its values and represent the interests of its people. Therefore, it can be quite difficult to change the attitudes and conservative views of the Curaçaoan community regarding the arts, and contemporary visual arts in particular, especially when this cultural conservatism permeates the mind-set of the students. For instance, as the IBB artist-mentors have commented, although most IBB students are receptive to and enthusiastic about experimenting with novel mediums and methods, some of them show resistance to more contemporary forms of art making and find it difficult to adapt these new concepts and approaches to their developing practice.

Although the IBB believes openness and flexibility can provide a strong basis for creativity, they have found that it can also impose great challenges. Since some students, especially the younger ones, are used to having authoritarian figures at home, in school, or at work, they are sometimes unable to cope with the flexibility and liberty that is given to them in the institute. Therefore, it is important for artist-mentors to develop this free energy, but also to channel it in a creative and positive way in order to prevent issues such as absenteeism or indolence that might cause students to go astray or thwart their artistic development.

Founded on strong democratic principles, the IBB has sought to give young Antilleans from disadvantaged neighborhoods the opportunity to engage in arts-based education. However, basic survival issues are still a priority for many families in Curaçao. Such is the case of twenty-two-year-old Kendrick Moesker. After finishing the IBB program, Kendrick was admitted to the Instituto Superior de Arte, a center for advanced studies in visual arts in Havana, Cuba. However, there was no father figure in his home, so he was obliged to put his art education aside in order to help his family. This situation has kept him from achieving his goal of continuing a more formal art education abroad. Within such a context, it is clear that external social and economic factors can pose great limitations to this arts-based organization.

Silent gains: The added value of the arts

Recent research on arts education advocates for the positive role the arts can have on the personal and social development of youth, and in the case of the IBB, this is no exception.[6] At a practical level, the existence of an art institution like IBB in Curaçao translates into possibilities for young people to improve their creative talents and skills. Most important, it also provides testimony to the value of the arts. This value can be measured by what the director of the institute, Nancy Hoffmann, refers to as silent gains: changes that manifest at a more abstract and micro level and therefore are usually unseen and unspoken by the majority of the population.

The creative education offered by the IBB provides youth with opportunities to learn critical, artistic, vocational, and cultural experiences beyond the traditional school environment. Furthermore, arts education can contribute to different learning styles and even lead to better communication skills and easier social interaction, as the case of fifteen-year-old Luiguino Brandao exemplifies. When Luigino started his courses at the IBB, he was extremely reserved and rarely spoke to his mentors, peers, and even his family. This withdrawn behavior led his family and teachers to believe he had a hearing impairment, and he was subsequently enrolled in a school for children with disabilities. After two years of active and creative participation in the IBB, the leading members of the institute have noticed a substantial change in his personal and social behavior. According to artist-mentor Tirzo Martha, who has always been in close contact with the young man's family and teachers, Luigino is much more talkative and outgoing with his family and is also more alert in school. Martha continues to observe that Luigino seems to be "more conscious of the fact that he needs to create his own conditions of possibility, and to a great extent his participation in the

IBB has led to that." Within the constrictions imposed by his poor living and social environment, the IBB has provided a space where this young man can develop his self-confidence and feel motivated and comfortable to express himself within the community.

Studies have also shown that for at-risk youth, the arts can contribute to reducing recidivism, stimulating awareness, and increasing self-esteem.[7] An exemplary case among IBB students is twenty-five-year-old Julivean Reigina. Coming from a poor and troubled neighborhood where he had been directly involved in a world of drugs, crime, and violence, and was even incarcerated at one point, Julivean had a passion for drawing but kept it to himself because there were no outlets where he could develop his interest in this field. In a personal interview, Julivean observed that the opportunity to participate in the IBB has opened up a window to the wider world, one that perhaps he would not have been able to have otherwise. The confidence, comfort, and freedom he has experienced in the IBB have given him a more positive overall outlook on life. Now he conceives of himself as an artist and is determined to achieve that goal. Moreover, the success he recently achieved by participating in the Stranger Festival, an international contest for young video makers in the Netherlands, has boosted and renewed his self-confidence while also giving him a sense of pride and accomplishment. "I never won anything in my life," Julivean proudly expressed after winning a prize. Even though he was just learning digital video techniques and had produced his first short film, his talent, enthusiasm, and perseverance won him a prize in the local category for his video entitled *Nadi Hasi* (translated from Papiamento as "Nothing to Do") and the opportunity to assist in a video workshop in Rotterdam, the Netherlands. The four-minute film addressed the issue of homelessness by making a visual analogy between the *chollers*, or junkies, and street dogs. Combining strong visual imagery with hip-hop music, Julivean's video demonstrates a strong sense of criticality by attesting to the precarious living conditions that are so closely linked to drug addiction and crime and by clearly denouncing the futility of a system that ultimately, as his video suggests, serves to perpetuate the hostility and deterioration of the social environment he lives in. Julivean's accomplishment with this video, which was inspired by his personal experiences and surroundings, shows how visual means can provide an ideal opportunity for self-exploration and self-reflection through the representation and narration of personal stories.

These examples demonstrate how through social processes like education, agency can be passed on to the student by stimulating his or her self-efficacy (that is, a belief in one's ability to affect the environment in a positive way) and providing this person with motivation to act as a potential agent of change. Furthermore, my research showed that the IBB is acting as a catalyst among Curaçaoan youth by promoting the role of consciousness raising and identity creation through its arts-based educational program. In other words, this art institution is facilitating the means for young Antilleans to develop certain crucial competencies necessary to function in today's complex society—to create what Sohelia Najand has called "new cultural citizens." Najand advocates see art and culture as pivotal in the creation of new cultural citizens, a concept she defines as "a study into the way in which individuals and groups can shape social changes and cultural innovation in times of globalization and cultural multiplicity and into the way postmodern individualism can be united with collective responsibility and cultural diversity." According to Najand, the development of new forms of citizenship can be achieved by stimulating certain faculties regarding personal development such as autonomy, engagement, and willingness to change, but also "the stimulation and coaching of passions as these create motivated, inspired and committed people."[8]

Toward best practices

In spite of being a young institution, the IBB has shown that art can be increasingly active in the formulation of social and cultural processes binding art practices to forms of social emancipation. Moreover, it embodies the art center as a significant site for learning and transformation where the artist assumes a practical, and perhaps political, role as educator and active participant in the civic development of youth.

Although the foundation of the IBB is specific to the Curaçao context, I believe a model like it could also be of great benefit to other Caribbean nations with similar conditions. Since most of these islands, especially the Lesser Antilles, are characterized by governments that greatly disregard the social role of the arts and do not see fit to create an infrastructural framework for artistic and cultural development, initiatives like the one proposed by the IBB represent a contribution by providing faculties among youth that do not currently exist or, as art curator and critic Charles Esche would contend, by transforming "existing conditions into different more aspirational and purposeful configurations."[9]

Although the need for this kind of initiative in developing countries might be all the more urgent, I believe that such an endeavor might also play a significant role in contexts with a more advanced cultural industry, for instance, in Europe or the United States. As an arts-based educational program, such a model could greatly heighten or complement existing opportunities regarding art education while contributing to the establishment of an alternative kind of learning—one grounded in creativity and imagination as fundamental tools for the development of healthy, resourceful, and engaged youth.

Notes

1. Hoffmann, N. (2007). Introduction. In R. Cornelissen (Ed.), *Wormhole*, 5, 2.

2. Oostindie, G. (2006). The study of ethnicity in the Dutch Caribbean: Full circle to Furnivall? *Latin American and Caribbean Ethnic Studies*, 1(2), 215–230.

3. Oostindie. (2006). P. 222.

4. Within the context of this article, the words *culture* and *cultural* refer mostly to arts culture instead of societal culture.

5. For more information, see Hoffmann, N., & Smit, J. (2004). *ARTESWA 2004*. Curaçao: ArteSwa Stichting.

6. Arts Education Partnership. (2004). *The arts and education: New opportunities for research*. Retrieved June 10, 2008, from http://www.aep-arts.org/files/research/OpportunitiesResearch.pdf; Eisner, E. (1998). Does experience

in the arts boost academic achievement? *Journal of Art and Design Education, 17*(1), 51–60.

7. See for example, Grossman, J. B., & Garry, E. M. (1997). *Mentoring: A proven delinquency prevention strategy.* Washington, DC: U.S. Department of Justice.

8. Najand, S. (2007). New cultural citizens are not born but created. In R. Braidotti, Ch. Esche, & M. Hlavajova (Eds.), *Citizens and subjects: The Netherlands for example.* 52nd International Art Exhibition, Venice Biennial. P. 203.

9. Esche, Ch. (2005). *Modest proposals.* Turkey: Baglam Publishing. P. 16.

IBERIA PÉREZ GONZÁLEZ *is an independent researcher for Dutch arts organizations.*

A hip-hop music-making program in Edmonton, Canada, successfully reengages at-risk Aboriginal youth in school and helps them establish a healthy sense of self.

4

The Beat of Boyle Street: Empowering Aboriginal youth through music making

Elaine L. Wang

ABORIGINAL YOUTH ARE particularly marginalized and at risk in mainstream Canadian society. In Edmonton, the city with the second highest urban population of Aboriginals in Canada, Aboriginal students have especially low school attendance rates and high dropout rates. Moreover, many are affected by poverty, homelessness, or racism, or they are involved in drugs and alcohol, gangs, and criminal activity. In 2003, the Beat of Boyle Street was founded to reconnect this population to school and help them establish a healthy sense of self. It does so through engaging students in creating, recording, and producing their own rap and remixes. Since its inception, the Beat of Boyle Street has won awards and accolades. It is a successful program that can be adapted to empower other at-risk youth groups.

NEW DIRECTIONS FOR YOUTH DEVELOPMENT, NO. 125, SPRING 2010 © WILEY PERIODICALS, INC.
Published online in Wiley InterScience (www.interscience.wiley.com) • DOI: 10.1002/yd.338

Instigating social conditions

Throughout Canada's history, the Aboriginal peoples have had to compromise their rights and way of life. Stripped of land and treated as subjects of assimilation, Aboriginals at one time had to surrender their rights to independence with regard to culture, land, governance, and resources to become legal Canadian citizens.[1] Further destruction of freedom and culture included alcohol prohibitions; barring of potlatch celebrations, pow-wows, and other ceremonies; and forceful placement of children into residential schools, distant from their family and community. The results were the destruction of children's self-esteem and irrevocable harm to Aboriginal languages and traditions. As is also well known, countless children succumbed to tuberculosis and became victims of abuse in this environment. Many children did not survive residential schools; many others became adults who relied on government welfare and had no sense of identity or belonging. Drug and alcohol abuse, antisocial behavior, criminal activities, and suicides became prevalent. Young people learn such conduct, and so a vicious cycle begins.[2]

Although the government of Canada has been trying to make reparations, the psyche of the Aboriginal people remains scarred. Aboriginal peoples and their needs are still often neglected; in particular, those who move to urban areas are often excluded from aboriginal collectives and the mainstream or governmental services.[3] In addition, Aboriginal people frequently face blatant discrimination, negative stereotypes, and derogatory characterizations.[4]

Aboriginals have a strong presence in urban areas. Edmonton has about 30,365 Aboriginals, composing 4.8 percent of the city's population and making it the second largest visible minority group. The largest and fastest-growing age group of Aboriginals in Edmonton is youth ages fifteen to twenty-four. In 2001, the school attendance rate of Aboriginal youth in Edmonton was about 52 percent.[5] Aboriginal youth in metropolitan areas are less likely to complete high school than their non-Aboriginal peers (57 percent versus 71 percent); the majority of young Aboriginal women drop

NEW DIRECTIONS FOR YOUTH DEVELOPMENT • DOI: 10.1002/yd

out due to pregnancy or the need to look after children, and most young men quit because they are bored or want to find work.[6] In 2001–2002, Aboriginal youth accounted for 36 percent of young offenders at in-house correctional facilities in Alberta; in fact, Aboriginal youth were four and a half times more likely than other youth to commit offenses. Furthermore, Edmonton is home to major Aboriginal-based street gangs that focus their recruitment on Aboriginal youth.[7] It is essential to Aboriginal students' self-esteem and desirable for society's welfare to keep Aboriginal students in school and interested in education.

Arts intervention

Established in 2003, the Beat of Boyle Street in Edmonton is a school-based for-credit music program that reengages Edmonton's Aboriginal inner-city youth in school by teaching them to use hip-hop and rap to express themselves. It offers access to and instruction in technology for students to make music and spoken-word poetry.[8] The participants have been affected by serious and deeply rooted social problems, including racism, poverty, homelessness, violence, poor parenting, teen pregnancy, substance abuse, criminal activities, and loss of family or cultural bonds. Many students are at risk of dropping out; several have had months to years of interruption in their education.[9] The program strives to make school a more pleasant, productive, and meaningful experience. It aims "to move youth-at-risk from activities related to crime and self-destruction toward positive alternatives."[10]

The project was sponsored by the National Crime Prevention Strategy (NCPS), the University of Alberta Recreation and Leisure Studies, and the Boyle Street Education Centre (BSEC). The NCPS is a government of Canada initiative that "seeks to develop community-based responses to crime, [with] emphasis on children and youth, Aboriginal people and communities."[11] BSEC is an independent charter school serving at-risk students ages fourteen to twenty in inner-city Edmonton.[12] It enrolls about a hundred

NEW DIRECTIONS FOR YOUTH DEVELOPMENT • DOI: 10.1002/yd

students, 90 percent of whom are of Aboriginal descent and 65 percent of whom have arrest records.[13] The school offers a core curriculum as well as electives in a range of subjects, including Cree language and culture, cosmetology, and music production.[14] Although brought to life and led by adults, particularly Brett Lashua, a doctoral candidate at the time researching popular culture, music technology, and leisure practices of urban youth, and Karen Fox, of the University of Alberta, the Beat of Boyle Street was initiated and inspired by students who expressed a desire to have a rap-music-making program.[15] BSEC already had a small studio, an orange-tiled room in the basement, but under the Beat of Boyle Street, the music lab expanded to a purposely built space in a new building.[16] The current facility houses multiple computer workstations with advanced software, MIDI keyboards, turntables, a digital mixer, and a soundproof recording studio.[17]

The Beat of Boyle Street consciously draws on the hip-hop culture to engage Aboriginal youth, for many have come to identify with rap and hip-hop styles, perhaps because they feel a connection with the alienation and despair African Americans had felt and expressed in these musical genres.[18] Furthermore, rap is regarded as a form of storytelling expressed by "historically marginalized, silenced and otherwise 'invisible' people."[19] The program was also built around hip-hop because it is a genre that urban youth are likely already familiar with. The program thus validates such street skills as creating beats, freestyling, and improvising.

Over the course of a ten-week school term, groups of six students work with instructors to write lyrics, play music, and learn the technology needed to make their recording. During the three years that Brett Lashua led the program, from 2003 to 2006, he worked with nearly 150 students, committing five hours a day for four days a week. At a typical session, students sit with the instructor at a computer station with audio production software to sample segments from songs, such as those by Tupac and Eminem. Students produce remixes by blending together, "mashing up," or "stitching together" existing ones.[20] Sometimes they draw on other genres of music, including classical, blues, and country. Other

NEW DIRECTIONS FOR YOUTH DEVELOPMENT • DOI: 10.1002/yd

times, they loop short segments of simple beats. Other options are mixing in video games effects, ring tones, and movie dialogue. The technique brings to mind the argument that "young people make and re-make culture through appropriating the cultural 'raw materials' of life in order to construct meaning in their own specific cultural localities."[21]

Once students have the background beat, they write lyrics, which are often poignant personal narratives about key people, places, moments, and emotions in their lives. Through this process, they represent their concerns, ideas, stories, cultures, relationships, and identities. Music making becomes a way of coping with, making meaning of, and asserting control over life.[22] For example, raps by MC Sound and MC Novakane demonstrate their keen awareness of the challenges confronting urban Aboriginal youth, including voicelessness and oppression by mainstream society.[23] At the same time, the raps embody a desire to unite the Aboriginal community and contribute to social change without violence.[24]

Another activity was rap battles. A recognized tradition of hip-hop culture, this is a "skill contest between two MCs who attempt to out-rhyme one another through dexterous vocabulary and lyrical challenges."[25] Such metaphorical battles are thought to have evolved as a way for people to vent their frustrations and express their aggression using words instead of weapons.[26] An example is the contest between MC Sound and MC El Jefe, student rappers from rivaling neighborhoods.[27] Although their lyrics seem to express threats, they are not alarming because verbal attacks on microphones in the studio essentially replace potential physical assaults on the street.

Despite students' attempts to distinguish themselves in these match-ups, their lyrics frequently reveal important similarities among them. The rap battles in this program often uncover social issues that reflect marginalized students' preoccupation with their perceived status and image. For instance, MC Sound alludes to his own learning problems due to being born with fetal alcohol syndrome, and MC El Jefe references the drinking of mouthwash as a cheap substitute for alcohol; interestingly, both rappers explicitly

NEW DIRECTIONS FOR YOUTH DEVELOPMENT • DOI: 10.1002/yd

identify their heritage ("Aboriginal-Canadian" and "Native") in their verses. The impromptu lyrics reveal significant personal information that can be used to broach difficult topics. Rap duels are also valuable because participants learn respect, humility, and collaboration. As a result of their contest, MC Sound and MC El Jefe developed a "high degree of respect for one another."[28] And when their recorded battle is played back, the resulting track is greater than the sum of its parts.

While the first year of the Beat of Boyle Street program focused on equipping the studio and helping students mix and record music, the second phase saw an expansion into the community as participants sought to teach their art to other youth.[29] Events and activities included student-led workshops, performances at an Aboriginal education conference, and live dance and talent competitions.

Program evaluation

The Beat of Boyle Street was "designed to connect with students through their own music . . ., build upon their own perspectives and understandings of the world, develop computer and music competencies, re-engage them in school, provide alternatives to negative behaviours . . . and provide positive motivation."[30] Indeed, the program had a positive impact on participants' attendance and interest in school.[31] Students noted making music or writing lyrics as "the most significant involvement that sustained them through their days."[32] MC Sound further articulates: "I used to be a pugilist, solve my problems with fists, but that's in the midst, you know? So I took it to passion and fashion and started writing rhyme after rhyme through poetry on loose-leaf line. This is what I like to do; I don't commit no crime."[33] MC Rasta P, a former young offender, shared similar sentiments: "I was trying to change some things around, and they took me in, and showed me how to mix some beats. . . . Now it keeps me out of trouble."[34] Participants also expressed a sense of personal growth and empowerment. For example, MC Novakane affirmed: "It gives me a chance to have my voice heard and make a difference in the community."[35]

The Beat of Boyle Street is also a success because students gained public recognition and positively influenced other youth. Several participants were awarded the Nellie Carlson Aboriginal Youth Award.[36] Others have volunteered as mentors at inner-city youth centers and even facilitated university classes on topics such as hip-hop lifestyle and its power for healing.[37] In 2006, the Beat of Boyle Street won a government of Alberta crime prevention award in the youth leadership category.[38] Also, the Alberta Recreation and Parks Association awarded five young adults associated with the program the Excellence in Youth Development Award for developing an arts-based recreation center.[39] The Beat of Boyle Street clearly inspired and empowered them to help other youth in need of mentorship and meaningful experiences. The success of the program therefore is magnified by the extent to which its participants actively sought to "pay it forward."

The creative and expressive orientation of the program is crucial to its success. Many of the participants' negative experiences have made them angry, frustrated, or confused. The Beat of Boyle Street offers the opportunity to articulate thoughts and emotions in a medium that engages them. Students' own words and expressions become a point of entry for critical dialogues about the popular media's negative, even racist portrayal of Aboriginals and major social issues such as racial and class conflicts.[40] Another strength of the program is that it draws on students' street skills and intuition for hip-hop culture; it validates competencies students already have developed, so to have it integrated as part of their school program is a way to engage these at-risk youth. This idea is captured in MC Rasta P's reflection: "[When] I heard about this music class . . . I thought it's just what I needed 'cause that's what I like doing, writing lyrics."[41] In addition, the method of remixing is effective because it allows students to experience immediate results without the frustrating and lengthy process of writing music or coordinating beats from scratch. This instant gratification helps to engage youth who have not experienced particular success in a learning environment.[42] At the same time, students learn to persevere to create a final product, such as a CD. Finally, as an intervention, the Beat of Boyle Street is successful because it is fun; it is structured play: "Sometimes it is important to just have a safe space to play, to create and recreate."[43]

Lessons learned and future applications

The Beat of Boyle Street suggests that a program for youth can be very effective if it is based on youth interests and is initiated by and created in consultation with the population it would serve. The fact that it forms an elective component of students' educational program may also contribute to its success because from the students' perspective, they are meeting required attendance time and earning credits toward graduation while essentially engaging in recreation and leisure. Furthermore, because classes are scheduled as part of students' course loads and convene regularly, the program is likely to achieve greater consistency of attendance than a drop-in or extracurricular program, thus encouraging stronger peer relationships and mutual support. Moreover, a school-based program is likely to offer a full progression of courses that accommodate students' developing skills. Finally, because it is delivered in an educational environment, the program can be regarded as formal, valid training for a potential career in the music industry. Students interested in pursuing writing, performing, sound editing, or producing therefore will feel they have the prerequisite experience to do so.

Marginalized or traditionally voiceless students must have a safe arena in which to develop creative expression. The medium of this expression should honor their prior knowledge and skills rather than be a rigid form of language or a generic activity deemed "literate" or "educational" or "valued" by the dominant culture. Youth must be in control of their own representation, in charge of shaping their own identity. Writing raps directly provided the participants of the Beat of Boyle Street this sense of agency, power, and accomplishment. The program demonstrates that popular culture and youth experiences need to be respected and can be highly effective in transforming classrooms and other environments into "more supportive, dialogic, and democratic spaces."[44] The Beat of Boyle Street reengaged at-risk students by giving them a project to focus on, a goal to strive for, a medium to express their feelings, a chance to be creative, and an opportunity to find themselves.

Notes

1. Canada in the making. (2005). *Aboriginals: Treaties and relations.* Retrieved March 21, 2008, from http://www.canadiana.org/citm/themes/aboriginals_e.html.

2. Canada in the making. (2005).

3. Lashua, B. D. (2006). The arts of the remix: Ethnography and rap. *Anthropology Matters Journal, 8*(2). Retrieved March 21, 2008, from http://www.anthropologymatters.com/index.php?journal=anth_matters&page=article&op=view&path%5B%5D=67&path%5B%5D=130.

4. Lashua, B. D., & Fox, K. (2007). Defining the groove: From remix to research in the Beat of Boyle Street. *Leisure Sciences, 29*(2), 143–158.

5. "Excerpts," adapted from Statistics Canada. (2005). *Education matters: Insights on education, learning and training in Canada.* Retrieved March 21, 2008, from http://www.statcan.gc.ca/pub/81–004-x/2005003/8612-eng.htm.

6. Edmonton Urban Aboriginal Accord Initiative. (2005). *Aboriginal Edmonton: A statistical profile of the Aboriginal population of the city of Edmonton.* Retrieved June 10, 2009, from http://www.edmonton.ca/city_government/documents/CityGov/AbEdPresentation.pdf#xml=http://search1.edmonton.ca/texis/ThunderstoneSearchService/pdfhi.txt?query=aboriginal&pr=www.edmonton.ca&prox=page&rorder=750&rprox=250&rdfreq=0&rwfreq=0&rlead=750&rdepth=0&sufs=1&order=r&cq=&id=4a2f6df81d.

7. Edmonton Urban Aboriginal Accord Initiative. (2005).

8. Lashua & Fox. (2007).

9. Lashua. (2006).

10. The Beat of Boyle Street. (2008). *The Beat of Boyle Street.* Retrieved March 21, 2008, from http://www.beatofboylestreet.com.

11. Department of Justice Canada. (2003). *Alberta crime prevention initiatives.* Retrieved March 21, 2008.

12. Leard, D. W., & Lashua, B. (2006). Popular media, critical pedagogy, and inner city youth. *Canadian Journal of Education, 29*(1), 244–264. Retrieved April 28, 2008, from http://www.csse.ca/CJE/Articles/FullText/CJE29–1/CJE29–1.pdf.

13. Lashua. (2006).

14. Lashua. (2006).

15. Lashua. (2006).

16. Lashua. (2006).

17. The Beat of Boyle Street. (2008).

18. Lashua & Fox. (2007).

19. Lashua & Fox. (2007). P. 149.

20. Lashua & Fox. (2007).

21. Lashua. (2006). P. 6.

22. Lashua. (2006).

23. Lashua. (2006).

24. Lashua & Fox. (2007).

25. Lashua & Fox. (2007). P. 152.

26. Lashua & Fox. (2007).

27. Lashua & Fox. (2007).

28. Lashua & Fox. (2007).

29. LeClaire, R. (2004). Keeping the beat on Boyle Street. *Young People's Press.* Retrieved March 21, 2008.

30. University of Alberta. (2006). *Youth leadership award for hip-hop crime prevention program.* Retrieved April 28, 2008, from http://www.physedandrec .ualberta.ca/news.cfm?story=4614.

31. City of Edmonton. (2003). *Annual report: Building a safer community 2003: Edmonton's Safer Cities initiatives.* Retrieved March 21, 2008.

32. Lashua. (2006). P. 3.

33. Lashua. (2006).

34. LeClaire. (2004).

35. Lashua & Fox. (2007).

36. University of Alberta. (2006).

37. University of Alberta. (2006).

38. Government of Alberta. (2006). *Crime prevention awards 2006.* Retrieved March 21, 2008, from http://www.solgps.alberta.ca/safe_ communities/ crime_prevention/crime_prevention_awards/Publications/Crime percent20 Prevention percent20Awards percent202006.pdf.

39. Alberta Recreation and Parks Association. (2007). *Awards.* Retrieved March 21, 2008, from http://awards.arpaonline.ca/current_detailed.htm.

40. Leard & Lashua. (2006).

41. Leard & Lashua. (2006). P. 253

42. Lashua. (2006).

43. LeClaire. (2004).

44. Leard & Lashua. (2006). P. 249.

ELAINE L. WANG *is a high school English teacher at Cambridge Rindge and Latin School in Cambridge, Massachusetts.*

Creative engagement with literary texts may uniquely and powerfully help young students develop critical thinking skills at a time of significant shortfalls in the U.S. education system.

5

Thinking creatively is thinking critically

Elizabeth Gruenfeld

AS I CLOSED THE INTERVIEW with three Boston Public School second graders and packed up my belongings, eight-year-old Melinda leaned into the circle again.[1] She reached toward my small notebook and pencil, stretched her body out on the floor, and began drawing a cat. This interview was an attempt to understand the impact of the Paper Picker Press (PPP) program on children's critical thinking development and relationship to reading. The protagonist in the interview story was a cat named Moe McTooth, an alley cat exploring the comforts of a safe home versus the vitality of living freely on city streets.[2] But Melinda's cat was a new invention. He had wide vacant eyes, wiry hair, and a long neck with familiar mythological neck protrusions. Melinda looked at the boys and laughed, saying, "Look, it's Moe McFrankenstine!"

Ezra and Tyrone laughed along excitedly. Ezra now picked up the pencil and drew another big circle, reminiscent of Melinda's cat head, on the opposite page. He erased it suddenly and, distinguishing his own unique creative expression, instead drew a small

NEW DIRECTIONS FOR YOUTH DEVELOPMENT, NO. 125, SPRING 2010 © WILEY PERIODICALS, INC.
Published online in Wiley InterScience (www.interscience.wiley.com) • DOI: 10.1002/yd.339

abstracted ghost with wild and tense uplifted arms. Beside it, he wrote, "Frank Monster." Frank Monster squinted toward Moe McFrankenstine, who was twice his size, and boldly proclaimed: "Me eat cat."

Cultivating critical thinking through creativity is the stated innovation of the PPP program, which aims to engage higher-order thinking through an arts-based approach to rediscovering literature through play. PPP starts with this premise: If a student is thinking creatively, that student is thinking critically because creative play is critical thinking. By encouraging students to stay with a challenging text, PPP believes it uniquely helps them remain both creatively and analytically engaged.

The program wields art making as agency. It aims to infuse students with a sense of ownership over texts and awaken their capacity for interpretation, while enabling students to connect stories with their own lived experience. The process encourages students to read, write, and respond creatively as they reimagine plot lines, characters, and endings. Students create sculptures, poems, and songs by synthesizing existing text with personal inspirations and creating something new. The program helps cultivate empathy through personal connection with characters and application of text to students' lives. PPP takes it a step further, encouraging students to ultimately create entirely new material from the old—that is, recycling. The process helps students explore readership and authorship as interactive processes and gain embodied mastery of the tools and concepts of literature, as well as varied art forms. PPP illuminates language as a trigger for artistic endeavor and reveals that no text is immune to creative intervention.[3]

This article explores analysis and synthesis, empowerment, and civic engagement as functions of the creative process, and it highlights historical antecedents for these ideas. It also explores the PPP hypothesis that critical thinking develops by employing creativity in relationship to literary text, by evaluating PPP programs in Boston Public School after-school locations.

Historical and philosophical antecedents

The PPP evolved out of an innovative response in 2003 to Argentina's economic fallout. There Eloisa Cartonera, a dynamic work cooperative in the colorful La Boca community of Buenos Aires, facilitated a partnership between impoverished cardboard pickers and Latin America's best writers to create individually decorated books out of recycled cardboard and unpublished writings. The project transformed in Lima where Sarita Cartonera, a nongovernmental organization committed to intervening creatively in issues of social inequality, founded a pedagogical program for low-literacy Peruvians that fostered engagement with literature by employing found cardboard and texts themselves as endlessly recyclable material.[4] The Boston-based PPP program, founded by Harvard University's Cultural Agents Initiative, found its inspiration in the Cartonera programs and applied it in a U.S. context.

PPP stands on the ground of predecessors who proclaimed the importance of the arts in democratic societies, to equalize participation and for their relationship to human cognition and emotion. John Dewey, U.S. philosopher and educator, emphasized the role of art in a democratic society as an equalizing force, where all citizens are art makers and in that way participate equally. Dewey specifies that the division created between artist and nonartist is a false dichotomy. "Each living creature is capable of esthetic quality," he wrote.[5] PPP gives opportunities to children from economically underserved communities to participate equally and powerfully in art making and reflection as active parts of learning, civic engagement, and humanness; humanness here becomes the innate right to feel, engage, participate, and be fully alive.

Paolo Freire, the influential Brazilian educator and progressive social critic, emphasized personal agency in one's learning as a means of social revolution. He cautioned against adopting external guidelines—those stemming from dominant systems of power outside oneself. Rather, he suggested that each of us might overturn social hierarchy by claiming our own freedom. In this view, freedom "is not an ideal located outside of man," but is instead inextricably linked to the creative act.[6] PPP finds footing in a Freirean spirit, encouraging children's freedom of expression, exploration, and creativity. By encouraging intervention in preestablished canons of literature, it fundamentally aims to show children, particularly children of marginalized socioeconomic groups, that no text is immune to intervention. By association, nothing in our society, our world, is immune to change and our impact on it. PPP strives to develop engaged citizens who can eventually use creative faculties to address issues yet unresolved, and perhaps yet unseen. Increased capacity for imagination, critical thinking, and empathy development all become fundamental to civic engagement, active participation, and social change.

Victor Shklovsky, the twentieth-century Russian formalist, highlights the centrality of art in enlivening human experience. In "Art as Technique," Shklovsky cautioned against habituation, arguing that it limits one's full capacity for critical thought and human perception. He wrote, "Art exists that one may recover the sensation of life; it exists to make one feel things, to make the stone *stony*."[7] Shklovsky suggested that art thrusts viewers and artists into greater clarity about the human experience and the world in which we live. Through defamiliarization, or making that which is familiar suddenly unfamiliar, we can prolong, deepen, and enhance perception. The process restores acuteness to the five senses. Defamiliarization through art renders us more fully awake to our critical and empathic capacities.

PPP seeks to realize Shklovsky's point. It is a container that teaches defamiliarization and prolonged attention to a text, such that unique perceptions emerge and the text holds less authority over time. The text ultimately transforms through the act of creative intervention and becomes a student's own. This act of transmutation leads to personal ownership, embodied mastery over textual concepts and tools, deepened empathy and critical thinking, and entirely new syntheses of literature with personal experience. These core concepts are the same ones that undergird collaborative development, mutual learning, peace education, and authentic leadership. PPP tools may have broad application to adjoining fields.

PPP aims to demystify literature through play. U.S. early childhood educators Lisa Murphy, known as "The Ooey Gooey Lady," Mary Ann Kohl,[8] and Bev Bos[9] defend the importance of play as a critical pathway to learning. Murphy explains, "I dream of a day when we say, 'Today everyone played so hard!'" [10] Contemporary U.S. educator Susan Hopkins also encourages play, imagination, and varied arts devices for empathy development in order to create more peaceful, democratic communities.[11]

These authors' research refers to young children; indeed young students are the focus of this article's analysis, yet PPP is testing its theories on students ranging from elementary to high school, across U.S. cities and abroad, and claims powerful impacts. As a result of creative intervention, play, and repeated engagement with the same challenging and well-written text, PPP theorizes that students develop critical thinking, sustained commitment to reading, and ultimately literacy development. These interviews with groups of young Boston Public School PPP students were my laboratory to test PPP hypotheses.

Creativity in action: PPP program and interviews

The PPP process begins with one well-written story as the entry point for creativity. Each program revolves around this same story repeatedly. As a starting point for art making, students are asked to reflect on the story, think about character motivation, and connect to it personally. Because the goals are literacy and critical thinking cultivation, teaching artists knit the art-making activities to the text, keeping students creatively and intellectually engaged. If a child plays with literature from the start rather than a more traditional sequence (read, analyze, then maybe play), the child's creative and critical faculties may be engaged simultaneously from the outset. PPP believes that this is a process in which children naturally engage. If they feel connected to and take ownership over a text, they will feel free to reinterpret it and cultivate their own voice. In a Freirean sense, they have a better chance of seeing their own power and continuing to use it.

In spring 2008, I set out to test PPP hypotheses by evaluating the program in three Boston Public School after-school programs. I completed three postprogram qualitative interviews with eleven second- and third-grade students, as well as individual interviews with teachers and teaching artists in Brighton and Allston, Massachusetts. In each interview, I read *Moe McTooth: An Alley Cat's Tale* with the children, followed their thinking using responsive interviewing techniques,[12] and observed their creative explorations. I sought to better understand program impact on student thinking, draw out patterns, and notice convergences and divergences among children. While interviews varied based on following the unique thinking, pace, and energy of each student group, there were convergences in results. Overall I found that children enjoyed the program; took ownership over stories; felt free to intervene, coauthor and cocreate at will; used imagination broadly and empathetically; and spontaneously synthesized disparate information in creative ways.

José is a second-grade Boston PPP student and the child of an undocumented family whose parents were recently deported; his grandmother and only remaining caretaker in the United States had recently died. Jose was understandably withdrawn and resistant in our group interview and grudgingly anticipated missing recess for it. When asked what he might like to change in the Moe McTooth story, he replied, "Nothing." Yet in the middle of the interview, he noticed that the first letter of each paragraph was capitalized and enlarged. It read "M-O-S," and he told me it was like the Spanish word *más*. His engagement was piqued by visual qualities on the page and connections to the Spanish language.

Immediately he personalized the story, deciding he would rename the story after himself. I wondered if he related to a story about a cat without a home based on his own trials. He chose the name "Joe McTooth," circling back to a similar suggestion (Moe McJoe) from another child. This personal connection seemed to engage José independently and collaboratively for the first time since discussing our mutual connection to Latin America.

In fact, most PPP students displayed imagination and empathy development, ownership over textual changes, and heightened collaborative creation abilities postprogram. Almost all students demonstrated high engagement with reading, choosing to read the story collectively aloud. The story drew out strong emotional responses in all students, who seemed to empathize with the protagonist. Almost every child wanted Moe McTooth to stop wandering after finding a safe home, perhaps connecting to the need for safety and stability. Another child announced weightily that the story made him "visualize," unlike his experiences reading in school. Visualization may relate to embodying and personalizing information, and it may be a prerequisite for synthesizing old ideas to create innovative ones.

It is possible that as empathy and imagination grow, the ability to predict cause and effect and draw conclusions becomes honed and critical thinking capacities develop. Understanding the relationships among empathy, critical thinking, and imagination merits further research, as does understanding applications to multiple fields.

When asked what children wanted to change in the story, most felt free to change something. This often resulted in changing the protagonist's name and identity (Moe McFrankenstein, Frank Monster, Moe McJoe, and Joe McTooth). Most students continued to engage with the text through spontaneous creative play even after the interview had ended.[13] The first group invented new cat characters, shown in the beginning interview excerpt. Another group played piano, did chalkboard drawing, and engaged in kinesthetic play after the PPP interview.

The third group was able to focus frenetic energy into cocreation. As we closed, Geneva and Estefania desperately wanted to recite to me the "Blue Gum" poem they had written together prior to the interview. They did so, and I asked if they wanted to make up a group poem here before ending. The creativity was my suggestion, but all children emphatically agreed. They shouted, "Yeah!" in unison, surprising me with their excitement. I suggested we go around and each say one word that came to mind about our time together. José offered "Honduras." I added "Chile." Estefania contributed, "Doo-Doo," and giggled; Geneva added, "Gum Doo-Doo," building on Estefania, and laughed more. Fernando said, "Calm," and titled the poem, "The Interview." Somehow this mishmash of words carried the meaning of our time together. As we got up to leave, José asked me if I wanted to come play with them during recess. Over this short forty minutes, resistance and freneticism transformed to artfulness.

Program philosophy

The PPP program aims to cultivate critical thinking at a time of significant shortfalls in the U.S. education system. The subsequent sections detail the philosophy and educational theories that underlie PPP and the need for such programs, that is, to help schools prepare children to succeed in statewide testing and far beyond.

Why the arts? Why literature?

PPP combines art making with text intervention to achieve active student engagement and the development of personal agency. PPP program coordinator Emily Ullman explains, "We're using the intrinsic staples of art . . . and applying that to literature and reading to try and engage kids in language as a creative process, in reading as a creative process, and in turn writing. . . . We're trying to get readers to recognize that the text doesn't mean anything until it's read; whoever does the reading does the creating."[14] The new creation, achieved by the coming together of authorship and readership, is intertextuality. Interpretation is creation, and vice versa.

We all interpret texts as we read, based on our experience; we bring our personality, gender, age, ethnicity, temperament, and momentary mood to the act of reading and interpretation. PPP invites readers to actively engage in the process and, especially for resistant readers, experience personal relevance, as with José. Ullman reminds us that by "bringing literature to life . . . you own the story."[15] The goal is letting go of deciphering what the author meant and instead taking on the story as one's own and creating something new based on it. The act of engaged reading leads to cocreation. Art making seems to provide scaffolding for engaging personal agency and creativity. It may give map coordinates on which students can develop critical thinking and reading engagement, track their progress, and see it reflected back to them. This approach may better invite struggling readers into the process than traditional literature classes do.

Cultivating higher-order thinking

Cultivating critical thinking through the arts is the stated innovation of the PPP program. Ullman rests her explanation on Bloom's taxonomy. In 1956, Benjamin Bloom led a group of educational psychologists to develop a classification system for levels of intellectual behavior important to learning. He identified six levels of cognitive domain: three considered "lower order thinking" and three considered "higher order thinking."[16] In the 1990s, a group of cognitive psychologists led by one of Bloom's former students, Lorin Anderson, updated the taxonomy based on relevance to twenty-first-century work.[17] The lowest orders in the taxonomy are Remembering, Understanding, and Applying. Remembering includes observation and information recall. Understanding refers to grasping meaning, interpreting fact, and comparing and contrasting. Applying involves using information and concepts in new situations to solve problems.

The higher-order thinking domains are analyzing, evaluating, and creating. Analyzing involves seeing patterns and recognizing hidden meanings. Evaluating is the ability to discriminate ideas, assess the value of theories, and recognize subjectivity. The highest-order thinking domain is creating, where we use old ideas to create new ones, generalize, predict, and draw conclusions. PPP argues that it uniquely cultivates critical thinking in its students by engaging the higher-order thinking realms.

Higher-order thinking may well parallel the art-making process, from seeing patterns (analyzing), to comparing and discriminating between ideas (evaluating), to using old ideas to create new ones (creating). The root of higher-order thinking "exists intrinsically in art" and art making, says Ullman, just as it exists in language and literature comprehension. In PPP, art and literature come together to enhance the cognitive development of underserved students.

This is where the PPP program may become a catalyst for social change. If students' confidence and commitment to reading are enhanced, it may reduce underachievement and school dropout rates and make some inroads toward chipping away at institutionalized poverty. "The creative process is what engages young people. It's what they like to do and it's what school is not enough of. So they hate it, so they leave it—[that's the] big picture," noted Ullman. That is the risk, and the critical need, for programs like PPP.

The MCAS: Challenges and opportunities

The U.S. education system suffers from shortfalls that threaten the cognitive development of a generation of young people. According to the 2006 Boston Public School District MCAS Massachusetts State Standardized Testing results summary, 48 percent of all third-grade students needed improvement in reading, 22 percent received warnings of academic failure, and only 24 percent scored Proficient in reading.[18] From 2006 to 2008, the percentage of low-income third graders statewide receiving warnings of academic failure rose from 17 to 23 percent.[19] By 2008, the percentage of students scoring Proficient in English Language Arts for grades 3 and 4 statewide declined further, and low-income students particularly showed increased failure warning.[20] The trend affirms the need for stronger early literacy programs and continuous literacy support for low-income students at the elementary school level.

Ullman frames the problem this way: In an effort to teach to their current understanding of the MCAS, elementary schools mistakenly focus on lower-order thinking skills such as memorization and information recall. She says, "80 percent of the questions we ask overall in elementary school exist in these beginning realms. . . . We're preparing kids to answer [lower-order] questions." This may leave students ill prepared to succeed on the MCAS and lacking in early training around critical thinking.

Ullman now teaches PPP facilitators and schools that the MCAS in fact tests for higher-order thinking. She highlights that test answers earning the highest points are ones where students recall details, but then make conclusions about the material and expand on what is there. If educators teach to an outdated perception of the test, students' ability to understand and question depth in literature remains limited.

Conclusion

While some suggestions for program improvement emerged throughout the interviews, most results supported PPP program claims. The children's spontaneous and persistent text interventions suggest that ten weeks in the program inspired creative innovation and play as functions of critical thinking development. Synthesis and re-creation were continuous. Engaging with the text seemed a pleasurable, accessible, and dynamic process. The results are preliminary but suggest a positive first-round impact on engagement with learning, ownership, higher-order thinking development, and imagination development.

Data are available on the PPP/Cartonera programs initiated in Mexico in fall 2008. In Mexico, unlike Boston, there were comparison groups to control for results, and school-aged children as well as high school students were tested. Those results suggest significant differences between program and control group students; program students across all grades appear to demonstrate heightened outcomes in terms of engagement, creative production, narrative comprehension, critical thinking, and commitment to postprogram reading and learning as compared to control group students.

While results are initially strong, questions remain. Harvard Graduate School of Education professor and literacy expert Paola

Uchelli suggests that the PPP program may offer new information to the field, since PPP uniquely integrates both narrative comprehension and narrative production into a single process. She asks, How does PPP develop children's understanding of literary concepts? What effect does intervention in a text have on reading comprehension at different grade levels? To what extent does text intervention help or interfere with reading comprehension of the original text? Does altering a story provide optimal scaffolding to further children's narrative skills? Finally, how does "recycling" original text help English Language Learners grasp narrative structure? The full implications of teaching text ownership, collaborative art making, and text intervention are not well known. Nor do we know what the impact of PPP involvement may be on MCAS test results over time. All are areas for further study.

Finally, it may be helpful to consider PPP application for children affected by violence or traumatic stress. The program indicates strong potential for helping children contextualize stress, express emotion, develop empathy, and practice multiple perspective taking. This intimates overlap with civic engagement work, peace education, and emergency education. Analysis of the PPP program is indeed creating new questions, new thought, and emerging possibilities in the field of education as well as in related fields.

Notes

1. All children's names have been changed to protect their identities.
2. Spinelli, E. (2003). *Moe McTooth: An alley cat's tale*. New York: Clarion Books.
3. Ullman, E. (2007). *Paper Picker Press at Gardner: Review packet*. Cambridge: Cultural Agents Initiative.
4. Sommer, D. (2008). *Paper Picker Press—Philosophy*. Retrieved January 19, 2010, from http://www.culturalagents.org/int/images/ppp/pdf/PPPPhilosophy .pdf.
5. Dewey, J. (1934). *Art as experience*. New York: Perigree Books. P. 16.
6. Freire, P. (1970). *Pedagogy of the oppressed*. New York: Continuum International Publishing Group. P. 31.
7. Shklovsky, V. (1917). *Art as technique*. Para. 15. Retrieved January 19, 2010, from http://www.culturalagents.org/int/biblio/pdf/shklovsky.pdf.
8. Kohl, M. (1994). *Preschool: It's the process not the product*. Silver Spring, MD: Gryphon House.

9. Bos, B. (1978). *Don't move the muffin tins.* Roseville, CA: Turn-the-Page Press.

10. Murphy, L. (2002). *A crash course in the language of wolves.* Ooey Gooey. Retrieved on January 19, 2010, from http://www.ooeygooey.com/mary/resources/tips/ess_ooey_tips_wolves.cfm.

11. Hopkins, S. (Ed.). (1999). *Hearing everyone's voice: Educating young children for peace and democratic community.* Redmond, WA: Exchange Press.

12. Rubin, H., & Rubin, I. (2004). *Qualitative interviewing: The art of hearing data* (2nd ed.). Thousand Oaks, CA: Sage.

13. Gruenfeld, L. (2008, May 22). *"Moe McFrankenstine": Evaluation of Paper Picker Press Program in Boston Public Schools.* Paper for Harvard University course on Cultural Agents, Cambridge, MA.

14. Gruenfeld. (2008, May 22).

15. Gruenfeld. (2008, May 22).

16. Soto, M., & Brewer, C. (1998). *Bloom's taxonomy.* Retrieved May 15, 2008, from http://www.officeport.com/edu/blooms.htm.

17. Soto & Brewer. (1998); Overbaugh, R., & Schultz, L. (2008). *Bloom's taxonomy.* Retrieved May 15, 2008, from http://www.odu.edu/educ/roverbau/bloom/blooms_taxonomy.htm.

18. Massachusetts Department of Education. (2006). *2006 MCAS results, Boston Public Schools.* Retrieved May 15, 2008, from http://www.boston.com/education/mcas/scores2006/results/boston.htm

19. Chester, M. (2008, September). Spring 2008 MCAS tests: Summary of state results. *Massachusetts Department of Elementary and Secondary Education.* Retrieved January 29, 2009, from http://www.doe.mass.edu/mcas/2008/results/summary.pdf.

20. Guarino, H., & Considine, J. C. (2008). *2008 MCAS results show continued mathematics gains in all grades: Declining results in elementary reading prompt call for change.* Retrieved January 19, 2010, from http://www.doe.mass.edu/news/news.aspx?id=4287.

ELIZABETH GRUENFELD *has worked with diverse youth and adults around the world using the arts, intercultural education and civic engagement tools, and therapeutic techniques.*

A community group, assisted by human rights lawyer Marco Abarca, transformed a deteriorated wooded area into an open classroom to teach workshops on urban ecology.

6

Aula Verde: Art as experience in community-based environmental education

Marco A. Abarca

AULA VERDE (GREEN CLASSROOM) is the name given to both a problem and its creative solution by a group of parolees and probationers (hereafter referred to as participants) who live in a troubled housing project in San Juan, Puerto Rico. The group transformed a deteriorated two-acre wooded area into a lush tropical forest to found Aula Verde, a community-based organization where the participants maintain the forest's qualities and offer environmental workshops for children and youth in primary and secondary school.

Aula Verde is a multidimensional project valuable for a range of disciplines. In this article, however, I focus on the role of art in its creative inception. To speak of art, I will not refer to a preconceived cultural form but rather to John Dewey's definition of art as a quality-permeating experience.

When challenged by Doris Sommer to explain the project from the perspective of art, I saw an opportunity to conduct an ex-post

NEW DIRECTIONS FOR YOUTH DEVELOPMENT, NO. 125, SPRING 2010 © WILEY PERIODICALS, INC.
Published online in Wiley InterScience (www.interscience.wiley.com) • DOI: 10.1002/yd.340

analysis of the project's conceptual underpinnings—that is, to explore how art is present in the project even if it was not conceived as an art project. In this analysis, I refer to the project's educational strategy of values clarification, which was developed by its precursors based on the ideas of participation and communication of meanings and values as stated in Deweyan pragmatism.

Following a brief history of the project, I address three questions that will serve as a framework for the analysis: (1) How does art work, according to Dewey's theory? (2) What worked, and what did not? (3) And what are the replication opportunities for youth development?

A brief history

The pilot project started in 2001 when the Civil Action and Education Corporation asked me to conduct applied research, based on a norm of the Constitution of Puerto Rico, which mandates that the penitentiary system be oriented toward moral and social rehabilitation.[1] While the term *rehabilitation* is not defined by law, it is defined in specialized literature as "the process of restoring an individual to her or his place in society by therapeutic, educational or correctional means."[2] A few problems follow from this working definition: it presupposes the existence of values and life skills for prisoners to sustain a crime-free livelihood. In fact, the profile of the prisoners and the social conditions of communities to which they are restored could render those suppositions invalid.

Based on facts corresponding to the status of socioeconomic and cultural rights of the correctional population, the project's objective was to assist a group of participants in defining their own place in society. Assistance consisted of providing participants work and education. The work was to improve the environmental conditions of a valuable space in their own community: a deteriorated two-acre wooded area within the property of Angeles Custodios, a local Catholic school. Education consisted of a core curriculum to facilitate the knowledge and skills for their environmental restoration

NEW DIRECTIONS FOR YOUTH DEVELOPMENT • DOI: 10.1002/yd

job and an underlying curriculum to facilitate a process of values clarification.

The project is based in the Manuel A. Pérez community, a half-century-old public housing project suffering from a high incidence of crime. Thirty-five persons took part in the trial periods, including thirteen persons between seventeen and twenty-one years of age. Twenty-three were hired, including twelve participants between eighteen and twenty-two years of age.

The pilot project was funded by fine monies imposed on Puerto Rico's government for violations to the rights of the penal population, a direct result of a lawsuit by the Civil Action and Education Corporation. The transformation of the wooded area was completed in three years. By the fourth year, ten participants, including five who reached the age of majority while in the project, founded an organization to successfully become self-employed by providing environmental workshops for public and private schools.

How does art work?

John Dewey addressed this question by way of compositional semantics defining art as a quality permeating experience.[3] Quality, he explained, can be captured through the senses, the intellect, or emotions, but a full aesthetic experience occurs only when these qualities jointly permeate someone's experience and reach consummation in the artist's communication of meanings and values to the audience through artwork.[4] From a normative perspective, the significance of an aesthetic experience, says Dewey, is to be judged by its effect on the individual's present and future and the way he or she contributes to society through the collective experience: "The moral office and human function of art can be intelligently discussed only in the context of culture."[5]

Consequently, to speak of how art works in Aula Verde when viewed from this particular prism, I propose that it is the process by which the aesthetic experience of restoring vibrancy and beauty to an abandoned urban forest connects with the rooting of ethical social conduct—not by some sort of moralizing indoctrination, but by the moral content of the quality of the experience itself.

The project participants' dedication and creative engagement in landscaping Aula Verde speak of their role as artists. Artists, said Dewey, are those engaged in intelligent and creative activities. In his own words, "The intelligent mechanic engaged in his job, interested in doing well and finding satisfaction in his handwork, caring for his materials and tools with genuine affection, is artistically engaged."[6]

Aula Verde, the woodland cultivated into a teaching forest, is the work of art that resulted from the participants' artistic engagement with the space. A work of art, said Dewey, is not a product (sculptures, music, gardens), but "what the product does with and in experience."[7] When a person interacts with a product, the outcome is an experience to be enjoyed because of its embedded qualities.

Finally, I will speak of "audience" as those who benefit from the qualities present in Aula Verde, particularly the children and youth participating in environmental workshops. An audience, said Dewey, is anyone engaged in the creative process. A work of art evolves every time the audience expresses his or her own meanings and values; in Dewey's own words, "a new poem is created every time one reads poetically."[8]

The practical connections between Dewey's ideas on art and Aula Verde's educational strategy is made explicit in the work of John Raths, Merril Harmin, and Sydney Simon, who used Dewey's *Art as Experience* as a point of departure to develop their method of values clarification. These authors asserted that humans can reflect about value issues and by doing so gain the most from their value-related experience.[9] They articulated the connection between experience and values in their values clarification method, which focuses not on values themselves but on the process of valuing.[10] To study the process of valuing, their method set to observe how a person chooses, prices, and acts on beliefs.[11]

However, values clarification is descriptive and therefore not committed to a particular normative framework; its precursors insisted that it cannot be applied alone if values formation is at stake. Therefore, Aula Verde's core curriculum used the ecosystem model to guide interventions in the environment and to reorient interventions if participants showed indifference to the moral standing of other persons and other living things and creatures. When appreciation of facts involved in the components of an environment is considered in relation to each other as a unit, the model facilitates a process of understanding interconnectedness, not indoctrinating it.

What worked, and what did not?

From its outset, the project planned to explore the needs and values of participants. Beginning in 2001, I explained the project to potential participants and asked them to relate its objectives and strategies to their personal interests. While all interviewees properly expressed their need to work, all of them failed to connect the project's objectives and strategies with their past experiences and future life plans. They needed the work, but the project's objectives were not of personal interest to them. To turn the equation around, if the project was to succeed, a connection between its objectives and the needs and values of participants had to be facilitated.

A psychologist conducted interviews and clinical research to study the needs, capacities, and interests of participants. The assessments served to benchmark individual and aggregate indicators under different variables, which in turn helped to understand each participant's process of valuing and to facilitate specialized help when required and agreed on with participants.

To study the process of valuing, we applied the method developed by Raths, Harmin, and Simon, which observes how a person freely chooses his or her beliefs and behavior from alternatives after due reflection and consideration of consequences; how a person prices his or her beliefs and behavior and publicly affirms them; and how a person acts on his or her beliefs with a consistent pattern.[12] They sustain that if these criteria are satisfied, it is possible to affirm that a value is part of a person's values system.

NEW DIRECTIONS FOR YOUTH DEVELOPMENT • DOI: 10.1002/yd

The following analysis applies Dewey's ideas on art to the process of creating Aula Verde and, more specifically, to the participants' individual and collective expression of meanings and values facilitated by the method of values clarification. Dewey said, "The experience is of material fraught with suspense and moving towards its own consummation through a connected series of varied incidents."[13]

The first phase of the project was oriented by the discussion strategy for values clarification. All discussions were held in group sessions where participants were introduced to drawings, plans, and documents submitted or personally presented by the project's consultants on natural sciences, landscaping, and architecture. The work of consultants was also discussed in light of literature addressing subject matter such as beauty and function, and conservation and development. Pictures, videos of tropical forests, and the work of the renowned Brazilian landscape architect Roberto Burle Marx were discussed. These discussions provided information with regard to the rhetorical dimension of the participants' valuing system, that is, on their willingness to publicly affirm their values and beliefs. Every time the participants affirmed a belief concerning the topics discussed, I would ask them to explain their point of view with an example from their lives.

The ideas submitted by consultants and materials discussed were developed into a collective concept named by the participants themselves as Aula Verde. While the transformation of the forest for the sake of it (as established in work contracts) did not make much sense in their life, the transformation of the wooded land into an open classroom for children became full of meaning. They conceived Aula Verde as a project about the "five senses of the environment." The term *sense* was not used in a traditional way but rather referred to humans, nature, economics, education, and health as components of the concept of sustainable development.

Art began to work in the experience of participants from the moment they became an "audience" in relation to the study materials, expressing their opinions about them and extracting what they needed from them to become creatively engaged in the project ahead. Art manifested itself in a creative and dialectic process whereby the participants learned from the educational material and in turn enriched the project with their own understanding of the material and its application to respond to their meanings and values.

Art did not work in the experience of participants' expressing skepticism, fear of commitment, apprehension of being ridiculed, depression, or plain disinterest in work. While most of these situations became less of a problem as the project progressed, plain disinterest did not. When disinterest was sustained throughout the project's implementation, art failed to positively affect their engagement and participation in the project and to contribute to the collective experience. In fact, some participants made it clear that they joined the project only because a correctional officer required them to work. Although the job was not denied to those who expressed and sustained disinterest, it is fair to say that the need to work did not stem from an interest in the particular job offered. Since there was no personal engagement in the creative process of conceiving the project, the quality of experience cannot be equated to that defined by Dewey as art.

To compare the instances where art worked to those where it did not, it must be stressed that the participants' needs and values are not static. The educational process awakened interest in some participants who at first expressed disinterest. For these participants, art worked. However, it is equally important to stress that needs and values cannot be taught or imposed as norms can; they can only be clarified. The clarification exercises provided insight into their own meanings and values. For those who failed to connect the project's objectives to their own meanings and values, art did not work.

While discussion forums were ongoing throughout the pilot project, other clarification techniques were introduced to inquire into different aspects of valuing. For instance, while the discussion strategies emphasized the rhetorical dimension of valuing, the dialogue strategies used emphasized the developmental dimension of valuing by exploring how a person freely chooses his or her beliefs and behavior from alternatives after reflection and consideration of consequences. The participants were asked in group or private sessions general questions like, "Which work tasks are you best suited to execute in the project?" Or specific questions like, "If you had to choose between two different pathways to be built in this forest, how would it affect the visitors' perception of the landscape? And why is it or should it be important for you, for us, or for visitors?"

The different dynamics between educational discussion forums and decision-making dialogue sessions made it clear that to prize and to choose are completely different actions. While discussions opened the space for new ideas, the choices made in the decision-making dialogue sessions reflected old patterns of power relations. Before the participants joined the project, they held different social rankings in the community. These rankings were imposed during the project's early phases of implementation. They were challenged as the project progressed and finally became expressed under a different paradigm.

For instance, when Juan, one of the participants, was presented in private with his Wechsler Adult Intelligence Scale-III test results showing a borderline intellectual quotient, he commented that the life expectancy of males in the underground economy of his community was twenty-five years of age. The fact that he had been engaged in such activities and had surpassed that age, he said, showed that he had the intellectual skills to survive in his community. Regardless of which work tasks Juan was better suited to execute according to his IQ, he was determined to play a leading role.

Much can be said about Juan's response, but first I had to take into consideration the context from which he exercised his value judgments. While values are normally equated to concepts of moral relevance referring to emotions (such as love, friendship), behavior (such as loyalty), or things (such as life), values are also part of underground human activity. In those cases, the problem is not whether these values are prized or chosen, but how they are lived out and how the corresponding choices constituting individual or cultural expressions affect those in a group or outside the group.

Juan's response encapsulated one of the project's challenges: how to take into account the participants' past experiences and use them as the foundation of new behavioral patterns and institutional formations. The ecosystem model became central to the elaboration of creative responses to counter the existence of human values resulting from marginalized or oppressive cultural formations. Taken as a metaphor to reflect and discuss social needs and problems, the ecosystem model strives to characterize the major dynamics of communities and synthesize the understanding of such systems—to foresee their behavior in response to particular changes and to prescribe interventions to achieve a desired result.[14]

As part of the project's tasks, the participants chose among three working groups. The first group of tasks included collecting and classifying samples of insects in different parts of the San Juan Bay Area and to use the inventory to make comparative assessments of environmental health. The second and third groups of tasks had to use the ongoing assessment made by the first group to plan the intervention in the forest and execute the plan. One group would build a greenhouse and cultivate plants to be introduced in the forest's understory, and the other would intervene in the forest to improve soil, water, light, and canopy conditions to introduce live species.

In the execution of tasks, the old power relations were expressed with new meanings. For instance, when Alberto was digging to demarcate a path for future visitors, a big beetle larva came out in a clump of clay. He made an exclamation of disgust and was ready to kill the "ugly" creature. Immediately, Juan and Carlos, another participant, commanded: "Hey, don't mess with my beans." I asked them about the meaning of the expression, and they explained to me that it is a popular expression meaning that one should not interfere with someone else's source of income. Their explanation was a sign that the project was heading in the right direction. The emerging normative commitments surfaced, under an ecologically informed paradigm, to transcend from the immediate experience of disgust caused by the appearance of larvae and moved onto more responsible yearnings. The old power structures responded to a new investment in the sustainable development of the environment: a community development project placed in a community school, a project whose objectives were to provide a fair opportunity to overcome the impact of living in a marginalized and oppressive cultural context.

NEW DIRECTIONS FOR YOUTH DEVELOPMENT • DOI: 10.1002/yd

Normative commitments would not have been interiorized in the participants' values structure or expressed in their relevant behavior if their experiences were not taken into consideration. Just as an aesthetic experience corresponds to a subjective process of valuing that cannot be taught or imposed, the process of clarification showed that the values Carlos and Juan referred to as life, loyalty, and honesty, which were important for past experiences in the underground economy, are the same values but lived differently in Aula Verde.

Seen through Dewey's conception of art, the project's participants became artistically engaged by interacting with their environment, making choices, and using their work tools and the living material available to them to make a forlorn space beautiful. In the creative process, they found meaning, reaffirmed their values in a constructive manner, and shared their work of art with an audience: Aula Verde's future patrons. Rare plant species and seeds were collected, nursed, and transplanted to form a mosaic of deep, tender, crisp green colors and contrasting bright tropical flowers blooming beneath the canopy and along the trunks standing as columns in this cathedral of Malaysian almond and mahogany trees. The product, Aula Verde, achieved the desired symbiotic and aesthetic functions, hosting over two hundred plant subspecies and niches for insects, amphibians, reptiles, turtles, and birds—a diversity ranging from water bugs to nesting hawks in the towering canopy.

The project's facilitation of aesthetic experiences cannot be identified as solely responsible for the project's outcome, its success and failures, but it proved to have a positive effect on some participants' values systems and relevant conduct. Here I must place the role of art in coordination with that of cultural agency to affirm that art was not only instrumental for institution building but also constitutive of it. The problem with the underground culture resides not in a lack of values but in the context in which they are lived. In the new context of Aula Verde, the participants act on their own values in a way that facilitates a crime-free livelihood.

To follow Dewey's ideas on art again, if the significance of an aesthetic experience is to be judged by its effect on the individual's present and future and his or her bonds with a particular social milieu, it is also fair to say that what Aula Verde did and still does in the experience of some participants and new members of their community is life changing.

During the three years of the pilot project, Aula Verde remained away from the public eye. But finally the consummation of aesthetic experience occurred when the interaction between the participants and their medium of expression turned into participation and communication between them and the audience. Aula Verde has not only been documented in several magazines, newspapers, and television programs, but its qualities have made it an open air laboratory for children and youth to enjoy environmental workshops.

Starting in July 2004, journalist Mimi Ortiz published the first article in a local newspaper. She titled her piece, "The Teaching Nature." Ortiz spent several days sharing with me and the participants. She sat alone under the mahogany trees, lying with bromeliads in the forest's pathways, observing the embracing amphitheater conformed by small *calatheas* evolving into *heliconias, strelitzias,* and then into the gigantic flowering walls of *Ravenala madagascariensis.* She arrived early in the morning and left late, when the forest's inhabitants can be recognized not by sight but by sounds. By describing all these emotions with her own sense of social justice, Mimi received the Overseas Press Club award in 2004 for her article.

Ever since, Aula Verde has received thousands of visitors each year, most of them children and youth who interact with the space and find their own meaning in it. The aesthetic experience lived in Aula Verde's forest, greenhouse, butterfly farm, and gardens has been well documented. Teachers are given educational materials to prepare students to visit Aula Verde, and the visit is completed with workshops consisting of four topics: the functional and aesthetic qualities of urban forests; the symbiosis among forests, humans, and animals; the propagation of insects' host plants; and the life cycle of butterflies. The project provides a unique opportunity to reflect on social and human change.

Replication opportunities for youth development

Aula Verde's pilot project was implemented in a community that is the second largest public housing project in Puerto Rico and a rough environment to undertake studies aimed at producing social change. In spite of these challenges, this pilot project succeeded, and opportunities for replica became imminent. The key to success for any replica is not to duplicate it but to adapt the previous experience to the new natural and social environment and the persons as a constitutive part of it.

While Aula Verde's pilot project was undertaken with the participation of community members between ages seventeen and forty-seven, its theoretical underpinnings are not age restricted and can be adapted for other population groups, as demonstrated in the first replica with primary schoolchildren. Both the pilot project and the possibility of replication opened the horizon of a long journey to motivate others to facilitate alternative community development projects.

The first replication of the pilot project took place between August 2008 and February 2009 when Rosanna Cerezo, a lawyer and doctoral candidate in Hispanic American literature, conducted a new project with a group of public school students between ages eleven and thirteen. Students were referred to us by their school counselor as being either "disadvantaged, problematic, or having special needs." In addition to the workshops provided by Aula Verde's educators, Cerezo used literature discussion groups and collective writing activities to assist students in developing teamwork skills that would prepare them to work as a group in building a small butterfly garden in their own school. The replication of the butterfly garden took six months to complete. Recently I joined Cerezo in the opening ceremony of the new butterfly house at the participating school. I was pleased to hear, among many positive observations made by teachers, how the project had positively affected children, both academically and behaviorally, and how the project served as a catalyst for a new dynamic in their school.

Aula Verde has served as a platform for the creation of new and creative community-based projects. As I draft this article, Cerezo is preparing, with the assistance of doctoral candidate in psychology Odette Escobar, a second and different project with children. Fellow professors and friends Mayra Vega and Mario Tacher are also preparing to undertake their own projects in Aula Verde. Mayra, who teaches communications at the School of Public Health of the University of Puerto Rico, is preparing an intervention with adolescents to address the joint problem of sexuality and drug use. Mario, a wholehearted humanist teaching biology at the University of Puerto Rico, is preparing a science curriculum specializing in community interventions in urban environments. All of them and I will be sharing the process and outcomes of these projects and will later engage in the evaluation of my pilot project's findings. Some of these findings were briefly discussed throughout this article and are summarized below as proposals for further validation:

- Cultural interventions that are not part of the culture being intervened will not make sense in the life of participants unless the intervention and its product are linked by participants to their needs and values.
- Although a person's needs and values system are not static, the system cannot be taught or imposed as norms can, only clarified.
- While values clarification is not and should not be normative, the ecosystem model can assist participants to place the discourse of the self in coordination with that of the others.
- Cultural interventions facing the existence of human values being expressed under marginalized or oppressive cultural formations may find resources in the ecosystem model to elaborate a creative response to counter marginalization or oppression.
- Cultural interventions in which normative commitments are established under the ecosystem model must take into account past experiences of participants as being foundational for new behavioral patterns and institutional formations.

- While the project's facilitation of aesthetic experiences cannot be placed as solely responsible of the project's transformative and empowering outcomes, it proved to have positive effects on some participants' value systems and conduct. Transdisciplinary approaches are always advised.

Notes

1. The Civil Action and Education Corporation is a nonprofit organization created in 1995 as part of the remedies in a class action lawsuit taking place at the U.S. District Court for Puerto Rico. The lawsuit started in 1979 as a process of penitentiary reform on the island. This type of structural injunction is not unique to Puerto Rico: in 1969, prison and jail conditions in forty-one states were held unconstitutional, and judicial interventions were directed at virtually every aspect of prison conditions. However, the remedies instantiated in the Civil Action and Education Corporation's objectives included not only litigation but also education and research on the problems and conditions of the correctional population.

2. *Criminological Thesaurus of the United Nations Interregional Crime and Justice Research Institute*. Retrieved January 15, 2010, from http://www.unicri.it/wwk/documentation/thesaurus.php.

3. Dewey, J. (2005). *Art as experience*. New York: Berkeley.

4. Dewey. (2005).

5. Dewey. (2005). P. 358.

6. Dewey. (2005). P. 4.

7. Dewey. (2005). P. 1.

8. Dewey. (2005). P. 112

9. Raths, L. E., Harmin, M., & Simon, S. (1978). *Values and teaching* (2nd ed.). Columbus, OH: Merrill. P. 286.

10. Simon, S., Howe, L. E., & Kirschenbaum, H. (1995). *Values clarification: A practical, action-directed workbook*. New York: Warner Booksat.

11. Simon, Howe, & Kirschenbaum. (1995).

12. Raths, Harmin, & Simon. (1978).

13. Dewey. (2005). P. 44.

14. United Nations Educational, Scientific and Cultural Organization. (2004). *Educating for a sustainable future: commitments and partnerships*. Barcelona: UNESCO.

MARCO A. ABARCA *is an associate professor at the University of Puerto Rico Law School.*

A survey of cultural activism that talks back to youth-targeted advertising and invites us all to do the same.

7

Fill in the blank: Culture jamming and the advertising of agency

Carrie Lambert-Beatty

FEATURING A PHOTOGRAPH of the beaming, bespectacled face of the Dalai Lama, Apple Computer's billboard near San Carlos, California, urged passersby to "think different." Until someone did. Then the billboard read, "Think disillusioned" (see Figure 7.1).

Vandalism? Artistic intervention? Or political action? Culture jamming, like this billboard alteration, is probably best understood as all three. Outraged by the creep of commerce into public environments and the cynical appropriation of history, culture, and ideals in the interests of branding, culture jammers are activists—typically but not exclusively young ones—who skeptically interpret commercial imagery, exposing the underlying ideological operations of icons, reworking them to produce critical commentary, or replacing them with alternative images. Recognizing that culture *is* politics—that realms like advertising and mass media are the places where identities are shaped, common sense is manufactured, and consent secured—culture jammers practice what author and critic Umberto Eco called "semiological guerrilla warfare."[1]

I thank the students in my course Art and Activism Since 1989: Culture Jam, at Harvard University in spring 2006 and fall 2008, particularly Christina Xu.

Figure 7.1. Billboard Liberation Front, *Think Disillusioned*, San Carlos, California, 1989

Photo: Jack Napier. © BLF 2009. Reprinted with permission.

"Billboard liberation" is a classic example of culture jamming, but it takes a range of other forms too. Consider counteradvertising campaigns like the one by *Adbusters* magazine in which evercool Joe Camel becomes gaunt and sallow Joe Chemo; or shopdropping, a reversal of shoplifting in which altered or alternative objects are left in stores to be puzzled over by consumers. Artist Emily Jacir distributed custom Christmas cards in New York City drugstores this way in 2000: They merged images of biblical Bethlehem with contemporary realities in the West Bank city, so that the timeless Nativity images familiar to Americans included the hovering Israeli army helicopters familiar to residents of Bethlehem in the present day.

Culture jamming also sometimes takes the form of more elaborate pranks, as when members of the group known as 0100101110101101.org posed as representatives of the Nike corporation, manning a slick information kiosk in Vienna notifying citizens that a historic town square would soon be renamed Nikeplatz and adorned with a giant sculpture of the company's iconic swoosh.

NEW DIRECTIONS FOR YOUTH DEVELOPMENT • DOI: 10.1002/yd

Cultural critic Mark Dery, one of the first to identify the tendency, called culture jammers "Groucho Marxists."[2] Humor is a constant element of culture jamming, whether biting as Jacir's or sophomoric as that of the advertising "correctors" who like to change the "b" in Starbucks posters to an "f." In the tradition of the French situationists or prankster-activist Abbie Hoffman, jammers combine incisive ideological critique with distinctly playful action.

Culture jamming purposefully confuses cultural expression and political activism, mirroring a world in which culture and power, image and reality are inextricably intertwined. But culture jamming is therefore open to question on a number of fronts. Does it preach only to the converted? Do small, symbolic rebellions really contribute to social change, or do they merely let off steam that might otherwise propel more practical endeavors? Is the political energy of relatively privileged citizens of the global North best spent on semiotic play—or in solidarity with people who are oppressed not just culturally and psychologically but economically and physically? While wars rage, are the corporate strategies of Nike or Apple the most worthwhile targets? And isn't culture jamming just the latest form of radical aesthetics anyway, all too easily appropriated by the very forces it is meant to counter?

Certainly no one would argue that billboard liberation or shop-dropping should replace strategies like community organizing, whistle-blowing, or engagement in the democratic process. But culture jamming is decidedly empowering. It has two crucial phases: first, becoming alert to the cultural forces that shape us and then altering or replacing their messages. With these two movements, it affirms freedom of thought in a world in which it seems media, government, and corporations try to do our thinking for us. It assumes, and for brief moments produces, an alert and skeptical citizenry. And it connects like-minded people into real and virtual affinity groups.

This matters for no one more than the young, for they are the most aggressively targeted members of society when it comes to corporate speech and marketing manipulation. Naomi Klein, the journalist who did the most to call attention to culture jamming and the anticorporate globalization movement of which it is one branch, recognized the corporate colonization of public and mental space as a primary social issue for the generation coming of age at the millennium. These were the youth who grew up with advertisements in their school bathrooms, sponsored TV channels in their classrooms, and business-funded research in their college science labs. "Simply put," she wrote in her 2000 book, *No Logo*, "anticorporatism is the brand of politics capturing the imagination of the next generation of troublemakers and shit-disturbers, and we only need to look to the student radicals of the 1960s and the ID warriors of the eighties and nineties to see the transformative impact such a shift can have."[3]

While the smart-ass prank will no doubt always have a place in cultural activism (and a certain appeal to adolescent energies), there are options that are both more generative and, in some cases, more legal. A number of practitioners have lately developed forms of what I call invitational culture jamming. Rather than hammering home a message, each of their actions creates a forum. Invitational culture jamming applies the jammer's creativity to the task of making space for other people's inventiveness to be expressed and works against the sly, aggressive, unidirectional, and commercially driven messaging that infuses so much public space—and so much mental space as well.

History

Traced back in time, culture jamming blurs into the long histories of graffiti, media hoaxes, activism, and art. It has an ancestor in the antifascist 1930s photo montages of German artist John Heartfield, who recombined images from magazines to deconstruct Nazi propaganda. It picks up the legacy of the situationists, who in the 1960s advocated poetic actions they called *détournement* (reworking the meaning of found images), and of the Yippies, who in the era of the Vietnam War specialized in using absurd antics to get media

NEW DIRECTIONS FOR YOUTH DEVELOPMENT • DOI: 10.1002/yd

attention for real issues (as when they gathered to exorcise evil spirits from the Pentagon). Culture jamming connects to the strategies of HIV-AIDS activists who in the 1980s and 1990s deployed visually powerful imagery like the Silence = Death logo and theatrical stunts like a "die-in" during a mass at St. Patrick's Cathedral in New York.[4] It adopts the path-breaking work of the Billboard Liberation Front, the anonymous collective at work in the San Francisco area since the late 1970s (thank them for "think disillusioned").[5] And it draws on the rebellious spirit of punk and do-it-yourself cultures: on the aesthetic—and ethic—of zines, sampling, and experimental music.

But culture jamming's history is best understood as connected with developments in marketing, advertising, and corporate strategy in the period of high globalization. Although name brands and their advertising go back to the nineteenth century, we have experienced a transformation of branding in recent decades in both degree and kind, according to Klein.[6] Her book brought attention to a shift in corporate behavior, predicated on the displacement of production from First to Third World and North to South, and from company-owned factories to contract manufacturers. These changes physically and legally distanced corporations from the making of their products. They also freed up capital for branding and marketing. The result? A name, a logo, and a set of cultural associations became quasi-commodities in themselves. Swooshes migrated from shoes made by the Nike shoe company to T-shirts promoting the values of energy and determination (just do it) that the superbrand was now in the business of signifying. The business term *brand equity*, which began being used in this period, recognizes this new emphasis on the value of a brand as an end in itself.[7] Corporations eager to shape and extend their most valuable asset— arguably now not factories or warehouses, but their name and the ideas it could be made to connote—developed the host of techniques we are so familiar with today, from buying the naming rights to stadiums (all too believably satirized by 0100101110101101.org in Vienna), to the infiltration of everyday social interaction by viral marketers. Meanwhile, corporate sponsorship, another kind of

NEW DIRECTIONS FOR YOUTH DEVELOPMENT • DOI: 10.1002/yd

branding, increasingly fills budget gaps in schools, museums, and public transportation.

This effort was disproportionately aimed at teenagers. If in the 1950s and 1960s the paradigmatic consumer was the suburban housewife, Klein points out that the 1990s "was a time for beaming MTV, Nike, Hilfiger, Microsoft, Netscape and *Wired* to global teens and their overgrown imitators."[8] Today's youth know marketing less as a series of bordered spaces—print ads or TV commercials—than as a kind of environmental ether—a tendency that accelerated with the mainstreaming and commercialization of the Internet in the late 1990s, which soon offered so many new ways to deliver eyeballs to advertisers.

The Internet also provided artists and activists with new platforms and new ways to connect with one another. It would become a crucial tool and site for culture jamming, which got its name from a mid-1980s broadcast in which experimental band Negativeland borrowed a term from ham radio (where jamming is deliberately disrupting a signal) to describe resistance to mainstream media through techniques like billboard alteration.[9] In the 1990s, similar terms began to be used for media sabotage and related forms of expression. The magazine and nonprofit corporation *Adbusters*, founded by Kalle Lasn in 1989, introduced the model of ads against advertising (spoofs like "Joe Chemo" that tried to sell a critical attitude rather than a product), as well as campaigns against media monopolies and promotion of acts of "mental environmentalism" like TV Turnoff Day. The idea of culture jamming met wider audiences in 1999 with Lasn's book *Culture Jam* and with the publication of *No Logo* in 2000.[10]

Invitational culture jamming

In 1953, the artist Robert Rauschenberg hung a set of plain white paintings in a New York gallery. To some viewers, the paintings seemed nihilistically to imply that art itself was over (earlier in the twentieth century, Alexander Rodchenko had made three monochrome canvases as the "logical conclusion" of painting). But to others, it was clear that Rauschenberg's white canvases were only the support for the real work of art, the way a screen is the support for a movie. As light changed in the gallery and viewers circulated in front of them, shadows played over Rauschenberg's white surfaces. It was as if there was a constantly changing image on the paintings—one produced not by the artist but by the viewers and the physical conditions they shared with the art work.

Some forty years later, the church and community leader Calvin O. Butts led members of his congregation at Harlem's Abyssinian Baptist Church out into the streets armed with long-poled brushes and buckets of whitewash. With these, they painted over dozens of billboards in their neighborhood that they felt cynically targeted the poor with ads for liquor and tobacco.[11] They defiantly took back the surfaces of the city by blanking them out. The congregation's anti-ads were monochromes of resistance.

Culture jamming implies at least temporary breakage; it updates the old image of the wrench in the gears. Most culture jamming forcefully inserts new messages in the place of existing ones. But some jammers have instead effectively combined the lessons of Butts's white paintings and Rauschenberg's: that a blank in itself is a powerful image and that what an artist or activist might provide is not so much messages as the opportunity for others to create them.

This was the idea behind the Bubble Project, begun by Ji Lee in 2005.[12] Lee, a designer who works in advertising, found himself infuriated by the way the products of his profession were taking over city streets (and subway cars and bus shelters, among many others). He came up with a simple plan. He printed out blank speech bubbles, like those in a comic strip, then surreptitiously (and, he admits, illegally) pasted them in strategic spots on advertisements in New York City. Later, Lee revisited his bubbles to photograph what pedestrians had written in the blank spaces (see Figure 7.2). The results range from crude ("I farted," a beautiful model in sunglasses now admits) to political (a sincere-looking character from the Grand Theft Auto video game wonders, "What

NEW DIRECTIONS FOR YOUTH DEVELOPMENT • DOI: 10.1002/yd

Figure 7.2. Ji Lee, *The Bubble Project*, New York City, 2008

Reprinted with permission.

country would Jesus bomb?"). Lee's bubbles turned the whole citizenry of New York City into potential culture jammers. The
results are by turns mundane and hilarious. Many bubble fillers
work in the mode of the billboard liberators (like the social critic
who has the army of lockstep android drones in a movie poster
telling us to "shut up and shop"). But the real point is that each
bubble is blank—which is to say open. Any completed bubble
might turn a corporate ad into a promotion for a local band, a
protest against consumer culture, or just the venue for a quick
laugh. And so each also advertises speech itself, reminding us that
we can be message producers as well as consumers. Like each bubble, the project as a whole is open-ended and invitational, for Lee's
Web site provides blank bubbles to download and invites anyone

to continue the project. "More bubbles mean more freed spaces," he says, "more sharing of personal thoughts, more reactions to current events, and most importantly, more imagination and fun."[13]

As Lee's interest in "imagination and fun" suggests, there is something purposefully childlike about the Bubble Project, from the cartoonish means of communication to the workbook-like character of the exercise. This is also the case with a project by an art team called Illegal Art, one of whose founders happens to be a fifth-grade teacher.[14] In 2004 they began to paste posters around New York City that looked like enlarged sheets of schoolroom paper—the kind with dotted guidelines to help beginners perfect their handwriting. At the upper left of each sheet was a single word, *God*, and a comma. Like Lee, Illegal Art posted blanks and then returned to see how people had finished the sentence (see Figure 7.3). Some respondents treated the word in its colloquial use as an amplifier ("God, I like girls with big asses"). Others read "God" as the addressee and completed the sentence as a prayer: "God, thank you

Figure 7.3. *GOD*, **New York City, 2001**

Photo courtesy of Illegal Art. Reprinted with permission.

NEW DIRECTIONS FOR YOUTH DEVELOPMENT • DOI: 10.1002/yd

for your son." "God, I've been looking for hours, and I'm still hungry." And, more snarkily, "God, please help me make better art."

If faceless corporations address us through their ads like some secular voice of God, Illegal Art asked people to address him (or them, or us) instead. The street advertisement was reworked as an invitation to think and speak rather than be thought for and spoken to. British artist Gillian Wearing had felt the need for this a decade before and illustrated it in her series of photographs of individuals on the street holding handwritten posters she had invited them to make. The title was, *Signs That Say What You Want Them to Say and Not Signs That Say What Someone Else Wants You to Say* (1992–1993).

There are other examples of fill-in-the-blank forms of culture jamming, less literal than these. Reprising Reverend Butts's gesture, a young artist named Jordan Seiler has found a way to break into the light boxes that hold advertisements in New York City bus shelters. He replaces the ads with sheets of white acrylic plastic.[15] (See Figure 7.4.) By day, each becomes a blank screen: ads turned into absence, the onslaught of commercial speech silenced. At night, because he covers all but certain portions of his non-ads with opaque tape, they become pieces of glowing minimalist art. In Oakland, California, artist Packard Jennings and the Anti-Advertising Agency surveyed the people who lived along a certain bus route to tell them what kind of advertising they objected to the most. He then designed images that were the exact opposite of each loathed advertising strategy. Then he pasted them over the ads on bus stop benches along the route, so that at least for a time, residents who did not like "ads that create false needs and desires" instead got the simple reminder, "You don't need it."; a wordless image of children peacefully playing with sticks appeared in response to residents' anger with advertising "that targets children."[16] (See Figure 7.5.)

Perhaps the most straightforward instance of invitational culture jamming is another project by Illegal Art. The title gives it away: *Suggestion Box* was a large cardboard box carried around the city along with blank index cards that people were invited to fill out and

Figure 7.4. Jordan Seiler, *White on White, 16th street & 7th avenue, NYC 8-28-08*, 2008

Reprinted with permission.

Figure 7.5. Packard Jennings and the Anti-Advertising Agency, Bus Stop Bench Ad Project, Oakland, California, 2006

NEW DIRECTIONS FOR YOUTH DEVELOPMENT • DOI: 10.1002/yd

deposit. Their suggestions ranged from plans for civic programs—having each New Yorker clean a section of sidewalk—to undeniably helpful hints (for example, "Take breath mints when offered").[17] Asking people for their thoughts not to hone a product's marketing, or shape a candidate's messaging, but simply because people have ideas about how to improve their common lives, *Suggestion Box*, later published as a book, demonstrated the concerns but also the creativity, humor, and ingenuity of ordinary people. Work like this shifts the meaning of the term *culture jamming*. *Jam* doesn't have to mean blockage, like a ham radio operator who jams a signal. It can mean an invitation to improvise and play—to jam like a musician.

Your turn

In lieu of a conclusion—which would seem anti-invitational—I close with some questions for debate, based on discussions about culture jamming I have had with students. They might be good questions to ask before designing a project or when reflecting on one after it has been enacted:

- Anyone with Internet access can start a blog, comment on a video, or post a message or video, complaint, poem, picture, or joke. So why do the artist-activists who practice invitational culture jamming seem to think we need to have more opportunities to express ourselves? What is the difference between doing so on a street poster or a Web site, a Suggestion Box card, or your Facebook page?
- Packard Jennings says he installed his anti-ads "nonpermissionally," and Ji Lee warns those who want to post their own bubbles to proceed at their own risk because they can be ticketed, fined, or even arrested for defacing advertisements with his stickers. That is to say, like outright billboard alteration, even some forms of invitational culture jamming are

decidedly not legal. Naomi Klein calls it "semiotic Robin Hoodism,"[18] but are these artist-activists justified in doing what they do even if it is against the law? In more traditional forms of protest, illegal activity like sitting-in is called civil disobedience. How does getting arrested for defacing an ad compare to being jailed for participating in a lunch counter integration?

• Not long after Gillian Wearing exhibited *Signs That Say What You Want Them to Say and Not Signs That Say What Someone Else Wants You to Say*, the British agency that makes ads for the Volkswagen company ran a series of TV commercials in which people held up handwritten signs expressing their inner thoughts.[19] For example, we have had opportunities to customize our Nikes or to create our own SUV ads on Chevrolet's Web site.[20] Corporations have appropriated not only the form of invitational initiatives, but the attitude of empowerment and freedom of speech behind them. What does it mean for this form of activism that the very entities culture jammers are trying to fight can take up their techniques and ideas so easily?

• For that matter, if your goal is to reduce the cacophony of desire-stimulating images by which we are surrounded, is producing more images (even blank ones) really an effective solution? The group IllegalSigns.ca and its offshoots have been identifying street ads and billboards that violate much-ignored city statutes restricting the placement of advertising. They then pester the relevant agencies until the billboards or street signs are removed. This is a more traditional, if also creative, form of activism. What does it do that the other examples do not? And what do they offer that this eminently practical strategy lacks?

Notes

1. Eco, U. (1986). *Travels in hyperreality*. New York: Harcourt.
2. Dery, M. (1993). *Culture jamming: culture jamming, hacking, slashing and sniping in the empire of signs*. Westfield, NJ: Open Media.
3. Klein, N. (2002). *No logo: No space, no choice, no jobs* (2nd ed.). New York: Picador. P. xxi. Klein was writing in the wake of the Seattle protests and before the U.S. invasions of Iraq and Afghanistan. Although antiwar politics have

(arguably) become primary for young activists since then and there has been diminished media attention to the anticorporate globalization movement, culture jamming and related anticorporate practices remain important areas of political dissent.

4. Deparle, J. (1990, January 3). Rude, rash, effective, Act-Up shifts AIDS policy." *New York Times*.

5. Segal, P. (1998). *In depth look at the early history of Blf.* Billboard Liberation Front. Retrieved September 5, 2008, from http://www.billboardliberation.com/indepth.html.

6. Klein. (2002).

7. The first use of the term in a *Wall Street Journal* article was in 1985.

8. Klein. (2002). P. 68.

9. Negativeland. (1984). *Jamcon, 84.* See Dery. (1993).

10. Lasn, K. (1999). *Culture jam: The uncooling of America.* New York: Morrow.

11. Strom, S. (1990, April 4). Billboard owners switching, not fighting. *New York Times*.

12. Lee, J. (2006). *Talk back: The Bubble Project.* New York: Mark Batty Publisher. See www.thebubbleproject.com.

13. Lee, J. (n.d.). *Manifesto.* Retrieved August 28, 2008, from www.the bubbleproject.com.

14. The cofounders of Illegal Art are Otis Kriegel and Michael McDevitt.

15. See Seiler's blog, *Public ad campaign.* at www.publicadcampaign.com.

16. This project was a collaboration between Jennings and the Anti-Advertising Agency, facilitated by the Catherine Clark Gallery in 2006. See http://antiadvertisingagency.com/category/projects/bus-stop-ad-project/.

17. Illegal Art (Otis Kriegel and Michael McDevitt). (2005). *Suggestion.* San Francisco: Chronicle Books. See www.illegalart.org/projects_suggest.cfm.

18. Klein. (2002). P. 280.

19. See McKervey, H., & Long, D. (2002). Makers and takers: Art and the appropriation of ideas. *CIRCA, 101,* 32–35.

20. This did not work out quite the way Chevrolet expected. See Bosman, J. (2006, April 4). Chevy tries a write-your-own-ad approach, and the potshots fly. *New York Times*. For an example, see http://www.youtube.com/watch?v=4oNedC3j0e4.

CARRIE LAMBERT-BEATTY *is assistant professor of visual and environmental studies and of history of art and architecture at Harvard University.*

Following the example of Taller Alacrán, from the Puerto Rican maestro Antonio Martorell, and Robert Blackburn's Printmaking Workshop, in Harlem, the author explores the studio workshop model as a way to democratize art.

8

Technepolitics: Who has a stake in the making of an American identity?

Christina Suszynski Green

LARGE MUSEUMS ARE VIEWED as disseminators of culture, voices for a community, and symbols of the level of civilization a nation or a people has attained. The more costly and rare the art acquisition, the more powerful the nation in which the museum that has acquired it resides. Philip Johnson, who curated for the Museum of Modern Art (MoMA) in the 1930s and 1940s, contended, "Once you could tell a lot about a community by its church. . . . It was the place the city took pride in. Now it is the cultural center, the museum as monument."[1] Thus, there is a long-standing tradition among diplomats to visit museums when abroad because they supposedly tell a visitor about that nation's people, ideas, and values.

In America, more than 84 percent of artists in the category of "fine artists, art directors, and animators" (visual artists excluding designers and architects) are white.[2] But curatorial prerogatives, economics, and sustained educational exposure are more determining factors in the likelihood that works by minorities will be

NEW DIRECTIONS FOR YOUTH DEVELOPMENT, NO. 125, SPRING 2010 © WILEY PERIODICALS, INC.
Published online in Wiley InterScience (www.interscience.wiley.com) • DOI: 10.1002/yd.342

113

purchased for American galleries in large American museums.[3] Thus, the presentation of American collections of art is a process often occasioned by skepticism due to a tradition of exclusionary practices of curators. I agree with the ethnomusicologist Gerard Béhague when he writes, "'The National Endowment for the Arts proclaims that a great nation deserves great art,' but what make the nation and its art great are first and foremost a recognition of and rejoicing in its people."[4] There is a misalignment of curatorial practices with what America has long believed itself to be: a nation of religious and political plurality and a mosaic of ethnicities with both an individualistic spirit and the possibility of pulling oneself up by one's bootstraps. Perhaps you have seen the cynical but sharply insightful episode of the Internet-based *The Pinky Show* in which a guest, a cat named Kim, reports on what she has recently learned about museums.[5] She speaks of trustees as the brokers who decide what is worth remembering and forgetting, throwing into relief how few have the privilege to define an American aesthetic.

The majority of visual art in America is authored by white artists not simply because the majority of artists (and curators) are white. Economic class also plays a significant role. The National Endowment for the Arts' report, *Artists in the Workforce*, shows that only about half of all visual artists work full time throughout the year, meaning that artists often live with partners who earn a more stable income, or they have savings and possibly resources from their families to help keep them afloat during times of unemployment. Also, about half of all visual artists have earned a bachelor's degree. Demos, a public policy research organization, reports in *Economic (In)Security: The Experience of the African-American and Latino Middle Classes* that only 2 percent of African Americans and 8 percent of Latinos could survive for nine months without work on their current financial assets.[6] And the presence of one bachelor's degree holder in a household—an indicator of the likelihood of entering and remaining in the middle class—is less likely to occur in the homes of minorities.[7] Thirty-four percent of African American and a quarter of Latino households currently in the middle class are at high risk of slipping out of the middle class due to the complete absence of a bachelor's degree.[8] Knowing this, it is difficult to convincingly argue to minority parents that their children would do well to pursue a fine arts degree. But a degree program is not the only way our nation can increase the visibility of American minority artists.

Through public K–12 education, there have been attempts in the past thirty years to increase national understandings of non-Western art and craft forms and to encourage urban public school students to participate in the large cultural institutions that abound in their cities. A report chaired by David Rockefeller, *Coming to Our Senses*, bemoans the state of public arts education in the United States and attempts to persuade the American public and legislators of the intellectual, social, and economic good the arts bring to our lives.[9] This argument is still being made today by researchers, teachers, artists, and philanthropists in the face of continued resistance to publicly funded excellent arts education nationwide. When budget cuts are necessary, the arts are often the first to be trimmed, being that federal and state funding has never relied on how well students test on their knowledge of the arts. And though this may not affect students whose parents can afford private lessons for them, those who must rely on their schools for their arts education are denied certain cultural capital at the very least when their arts programs are scaled back or terminated. It is perhaps no surprise, then, that the numbers of minorities, comprising about 42 percent of public school students,[10] who claim they earn their livings as artists has gone almost unchanged in fifteen years—10 percent, 5 percent of whom are black.[11]

It is clear that the common arguments for the arts in the schools are not getting through to legislators or helping those most in need of a free arts education, the focus generally being on the cognitive benefits of the arts, the inherently peace-generating qualities of the arts, and the importance of raising future consumers of arts who will keep aspects of the entertainment industry, like Broadway, alive and well. The answers may not reside with public education. There are intriguing and convincing examples of how artists, philanthropists, educators, and curators are making inroads by sidestepping boards of education all together.

NEW DIRECTIONS FOR YOUTH DEVELOPMENT • DOI: 10.1002/yd

Philip Nausbaum, a former folklorist with the Minnesota State Arts Board, recalls the strategies he devised to help folk artists through the grant application process, which is necessary for exposure in the United States but hostile to many who struggle with English:

In many cases, grants to underserved constituents rely on folklorists working closely with applicants to produce convincing proposals for panel review. Such one-on-one promotion of grant programs is especially helpful to those who do not possess the English literacy skills required to undertake the application process solo. I recall sitting with artists who spoke halting English and explaining to them the dimensions of grant programs. Sometimes we communicated using a combination of English and Spanish; occasionally I would communicate through an interpreter. It takes patience, but it is possible to overcome language obstacles when there is a commitment to communicating. Many folklorists at state arts agencies relate similar experiences.[12]

So even though an increasing number of grants may be available to artists of color, there is not always adequate support provided to artists so they may complete the applications for the funds. Nausbaum's strategy is an excellent model for overcoming this barrier and a lesson in the patience democracy requires.

To give another sampling of how the minorities are finding success in the arts, an affiliate group of MoMA, Friends of Education, was founded in 1993 to raise money for the museum in order to purchase more works by African Americans and encourage more participation by the African American community in MoMA. This strategy acknowledges that museums possess value for all Americans, and yet it states that the museum experience would be improved by the increased curating of works by African Americans—people who have been responsible for shaping so much of American identity at home and abroad. Artists who have benefited from such efforts are Kerry James Marshall and Willie Cole. Marshall, who was awarded a Studio Museum in Harlem fellowship in 1985 and a McArthur fellowship in 1997, paints works that speak to an African American experience and politicize that experience by dialogue with and pushing back against traditional Western aesthetics. His work *Study for Blue Water, Silver Moon* (1991) was acquired by the museum in 2003, and though one may think Marshall did not need the help of an organization like Friends of Education once having received a McArthur fellowship, Robert Blackburn is a good example of why such organizations play an important role in the positioning of minority perspectives in museums. Blackburn, to whom we will return later, also received a McArthur fellowship, but his works are nowhere in MoMA's collection, even though this African American master printmaker trained scores of artists from around the world whose works are represented in the museum's collection.

Exit Art in Manhattan is another organization that has toiled since 1984 to make the curatorial process more democratic, recently initiating "conceptplus," a program that solicits submissions from hundreds of burgeoning international artists with social and political messages. The goal of these artists and curatorial movements is not to accept the traditional and increasingly extinct missions of museums, which strip politics from their daily operations and interpretive presentations, but rather to question supposed "obligation[s] to further the audience's spiritual growth"[13] and the idea that fine art may be reduced to truth and beauty,[14] consolation,[15] or "location based entertainment."[16]

The presentation of this dilemma is designed first to shed light on the complexity of achieving democracy in the arts, but it is also organized to draw the reader's attention to programs that are little recognized in America for the excellent work they do. And since our youth are not being served by public K–12 schools equally, in the arts or other subjects for that matter, what is education's role in the creation of future visual artists? The strategies already noted are certainly doing necessary and good work, though one model that has struck me as underused in the United States is the workshop model because it aims not only to develop the technical skills of budding artists but these other challenges mentioned: the need to overcome language barriers when raising money, tapping into the knowledge of more seasoned artists when learning how to promote one's art, and participating in a collective that has the goal of selling art. Known as *ateliers* in French and *talleres* in Spanish, workshops are not generally affiliated with school districts, conservatories, colleges, or universities but are run independently under the direction of a master artist.

Workshops were the means by which artists learned their trades in ancient Arabia and the Qing dynasty in China and Renaissance Europe, and either a sole patron or the profits from services rendered or works sold kept them operating. Today in the United States and in Puerto Rico, workshops may apply as nonprofit organizations for grants issued by the government or private foundations in order to subsidize basic operating expenses. Such grants are available in large part due to the fact that in both cultures, art is deemed an essential good from which the public benefits, whether or not it turns a profit.

My aim is to share glimpses of such workshops by opening up my interviews to my readers because I have never been convinced by the power of this system more than when I am speaking to or observing someone who is part of one. I conducted a set of interviews about two such movements in San Juan and New York City in order to learn what makes workshops special and where they depart from public K–12 schools, conservatories, and colleges but also how their methodologies attracted young people of color with no formal arts training, developed them as artist-apprentices, offered them financial support, and ushered them into the formal arts market as practicing artists.

The first interview is with Antonio Martorell, a seventy-year-old Puerto Rican maestro whose craft is rooted in printmaking. Martorell began his advanced visual arts training after taking a degree in international foreign relations at George Washington University. Over the years, these experiences, in addition to his personal politics, have charged his work with social and political commentary, which has earned him a reputation as a dissident, inciting anger, awe, and inspiration among fellow Puerto Ricans and Americans alike. At times, funding has been denied him due to his politics; at others, it has been dropped in his lap due to his commitment to youth. His unapologetic separatist views have led to his house being set ablaze by opponents, and yet his life's corpus has earned him a fellowship at Harvard with the David Rockefeller Center for Latin American Studies. Martorell, who naturally teaches as he speaks and works, has a long history of working with young people in both Puerto Rico and the United States. This has included work at group homes, public K–12 schools, and museums as a resident artist. But it has also involved community projects and, most historically significant, his legendary workshop, Taller Alacrán, which opened in 1968. There is almost nothing written in English about Taller Alacrán, and yet it addressed so many of the woes and dreams of Americans who have been searching for arts education solutions since the 1970s. More to the point, many apprentices of Taller Alacrán found a home when public school was not addressing their needs: they learned a marketable craft, received payment for their work, went on to open their own workshops, and became artists in their own right. Taller Alacrán lasted only four years (1968–1972).

CSG: What became of the apprentices in your workshop?

AM: Roberto Antonio Cortés was one of the school dropouts. He came from Aidonito up in the hills at sixteen years old. Twenty years later I caught up with him in Cayey. He was a cabinetmaker. And then he started doing frames for me. Many of them [the apprentices]—at least two—went on to be well known: Carmelo Martinez and Manuel Garcia. My workshop gave birth to many workshops on the island and in New York. They started as small, independent workshops because we didn't just do graphics; we did crafts like fabric, papier mâché, jewelry, wallpaper. One became an assistant to a senator in New Jersey; some went into fashion design. The intention was never to produce artists but to make them aware of the political and social situation and to make them be able to go beyond the limitations of poverty and vice within their communities. Some went back to school, but most went on to the workforce. Some of the young artists went on to teaching in colleges, but the whole thing was not about going back to school either. It was a time when schools and universities were very much in disgrace because they didn't fit our needs. What we wanted to do was provide alternatives. The kids didn't feel they were getting anything out of education. They felt a need to interact more with society. They were bored. School now and then is like a long, protracted period of being at the receiving end of something. And I could identify with that because during my education, I was very resentful. I learned too early that this was all about faking it and about power. So although I went through five years of university training, I found my life's vocation in a workshop doing things I believed in. You don't learn by being on the receiving end. You help someone by working with what he or she does best and by doing it from the start.

The workshop was mostly about filling the day with joyous work. Knowing that what you're doing makes you feel alive and changing matter, transforming matter, making something out of something else . . . your whole life becomes a metaphor.

CSG: What happened when the workshop lost its funding and had to close?

AM: I started to travel and give silkscreen workshops to people living under political dictatorships.

CSG: Does art and the creation of it give one a political voice?

AM: Art is always a very personal affair, but so is politics. So when I take politics as a direct or indirect part of my work, it's necessary because I believe in the necessity of art. The thing is it cannot be forced—you have to come from the depth of feeling, of really identifying with something you believe in.

Mine is such a political country. Being as yet a colony of the United States at this late stage of history, I can never shy away from that too long, and it creeps up in my work one way or another. . . . Since I have the nerve to express it by image or work or act, it's an inner necessity. Art is not an end itself; it's an instrument.

CSG: There are some people who would dispute that, such as John Dewey—that it [art] has intrinsic benefits.

AM: But regardless of our good intentions, this society is built in such a way that very few people can really dedicate themselves to art. It's not meant to be necessary, but you can relate to it, you can practice it, you can know it, you can be a recreating spectator. And then if you have practiced art at any time in your life, that remains with you, that gives you instruments to deal with life. As an artist I will always favor people doing art because it's what gives me pleasure. I imagine it gives pleasure to everyone, so I'm a big advocator of art making, no matter what you do in life. But that is very seldom achieved, so if you can get them acquainted enough to start so that they can vicariously or through memory, they can enjoy art and live it in whatever way they're able to. I do believe that everyone is an artist in potential—of whatever art—not only painting: music, literature, dance, whatever. We all have it in us but very few of us have the opportunities, unfortunately. . . .

CSG: What do you think the role of the government should be in the cultivation of aesthetic knowledge?

AM: It should be equal to the amount they devote to science because they both deal with knowledge and with the betterment of humanity. Unfortunately, they don't think so. Art is seen still as an ornament, decoration, or investment. The dark side to the high prices of art is that it builds and enhances the economic value of art and not its real value, so you get a lot of young artists who want to make it and they feel distressed, frustrated, done for if they don't sell at high prices early on in their careers. They feel like failures. The greatest benefit of art is doing it, ha ha. And any two artists will tell you that if you get something for it, fine, so you can do more and have more pleasure! Ha ha. . . .

CSG: In the United States, there's been an argument for the last thirty years or so about what the role is that the government should play in funding the arts and the role the arts should play in education. And I wonder what exactly the point of the argument is from the perspective of artists. Does it need to be in the schools? Are public schools the best places to have arts education? Do they belong in community centers? Could it be anywhere? Is there such a thing as a best place?

AM: Any opportunity is a good opportunity for art making and art appreciation and art living. Any. I wouldn't restrict it to any environment. I think the more the better and the earlier the better. It needs to start at the home.

What I learned from Martorell is that a workshop can serve many purposes. More than teaching a person a craft, workshops cultivate the entire artist, demonstrating how fundraising is done, valuing politics as a part of one's artistic identity, teaching by example the value of hard and persistent work, teaching young artists how to gauge the worth of their work and pursue quality over celebrity, showing how to make a living as an artist, and being a living example of the symbiotic relationship between community and art. His collaborator, Carmelo Sobrino, opened his own workshop in the 1970s; he is an accomplished artist to this day and continues to work with young people.

In much the same vein, Robert Blackburn started the Printmaking Workshop (PMW) in Harlem during the Great Depression as a collective with a vision of equality in the arts. Many artists who trained in his workshop are household names today, and because his workshop had such a powerful influence on the art of American printmaking, Elizabeth Foundation for the Arts, a nonprofit organization, carries on his work in a studio in Hell's Kitchen. I interviewed Deborah Cheney in 2008 in order to get a sense of the importance of his work to American and minority artists in America. Cheney is the program officer of the Robert Blackburn Printmaking Workshop (RBPMW):

CSG: What was your relationship with Bob Blackburn? How did you meet, what was he like, how were you inspired by him in the work you do today?

DC: I personally did not have the pleasure of meeting Bob. However, running his workshop and being around so many former workshop members and artists who knew him and share stories about him makes me feel like I knew him. His legacy as a master printer and icon in the print world is inspiring for me as a printer and one who is working to continue his workshop's mission.

CSG: Did he ever declare a mission in creating his workshop?

DC: Yes, as an African American who grew up in Harlem in the '20s and '30s and lived in a time of severe segregation, he made it his mission to create a community print shop where anyone, regardless of gender, race, or financial situation, would be able to come and learn about and create prints.

CSG: How did his workshop and method change the New York City, U.S., and global arts scene, in your opinion?

DC: Through Bob's inspiration, influence, and generosity, print-makers in New York City, as well as around the globe, set up shops using the PMW and Bob's mission as a model, thus educating the public about printmaking and spreading the influence of print media to the art scene. Also, Bob being the first master printer at ULAE and introducing artists like Rauschenberg and Jasper Johns to lithography placed printmaking on the map, rising to a higher level of fine art.

CSG: Is a workshop like BB's [Bob Blackburn's] replicable?

DC: Yes and no. You can have a shop with the same mission, facilities, activities, classes, and it can be a very wonderful vibrant studio. But Bob himself cannot be replicated. We are fortunate to have his spirit here within the equipment and pictures and memories and stories shared by former PMW members.

CSG: What was so special about BB's workshop that the Elizabeth Foundation continues its work today?

DC: Its longevity—being the longest-running cooperative workshop in the country; the impact that Bob had on printmaking, the reputation of the PMW as being a haven for all printmakers to make art and learn from Bob.

CSG: What did BB's workshop provide that public schools did not or could not?

DC: The workshop provided a community of printmakers and artists that range in all skill levels from very beginner with little to no knowledge to master printers who used the workshop as their collaborating and editioning studio. As an open workshop, ideas, techniques, and opportunities are shared, so the amount of knowledge one would be accessible to was immense.

CSG: Please talk about the role the Printmaking Workshop plays in ushering minorities into and maintaining their arts careers.

DC: [It] always has been a very multicultural/national community at the workshop, which is inviting and attractive and welcoming to minorities. Founded by Bob as a welcome place for minorities to come make art, we offer support by giving them opportunities to apply for fellowships, be involved in open studio events and member shows of their work. Also we help with obtaining and retaining artists' visas by writing letters of support.

CSG: What aspects apart from experiences like the Printmaking Workshop are important for minorities to gain more of a voice in mainstream arts venues, such as museums and galleries?

DC: Research and target fellowship, exhibition, and grant opportunities specific to minority artists, but don't just limit oneself only to these targeted sources of support. Get yourself and your art out there, everywhere, meeting people. The more you can promote yourself, the more you can have others promote you and your art.

CSG: If you could give advice to the New York City DOE, the New York State Education Department, or the federal government regarding arts education, what would it be?

DC: It is imperative that art education not be cut out of students' curriculum. It is an invaluable resource for empowering young people to exercise their creativity, giving an outlet for expression and self-exploration. The value of the arts must be taught at an early age.

CSG: Why is the Printmaking Workshop important for local communities?

DC: Especially now in this dismal economic climate, collaborating and supporting each other locally is important. Working together pulling resources makes the dollar stretch further, enabling projects on a larger scale to become a reality. Working together is the only way organizations are going to survive economic crises. It's important for the morale and the health of a community. The success of working together will show funding institutions your importance as an organization and will give a better chance of continued funding.

What is notable about the work at Elizabeth Foundation and the RBPMW is that they represent the workshop model at its best. They offer classes to the public, accept members based on an application process, offer studio space and supplies, exposure and professional development to those members, offer internships, and generate an audience for the work they do.

Workshops are not the only answer to democratizing American art museums. Workshops and the various other efforts I have highlighted, along with many other small movements and efforts, in this article demonstrate that the public school system is not the only domain in which we need to be focusing our energies. When we discuss a better delivery system for our democratic ideals, we do well to be open to the possibility that the best answers may not always be found in the use of public money. The past thirty years of debate about why urban public schools are shortchanged when it comes to arts education are likely to continue for another thirty years. And although I strongly believe sequential arts courses belong in every school and the arts deserve to be seamlessly integrated into all disciplines, our hands do not have to be tied while we participate in these debates.

Notes

1. Meyer, K. E. (1979). *The art museum: Power, money, ethics.* New York: Morrow. P. 130.

2. National Endowment for the Arts. (May, 2008). *Artists in the workforce: 1990–2005.* Washington, DC: Office of Research and Analysis.

3. For the purposes of this article, the expression "American gallery" refers to collections of art that are deemed by curators to be quintessentially American and aim to form a cohesive representation of what it means to be American. Although African American, Latin American, and Asian American galleries also exist, my interest is in the demarginalization of works by minorities and more inclusion in regular American galleries. Studies show that museums are starting to move in this direction. Institute of Museum and Library Services. (2004, July 16). *African American history and culture in museums: Strategic crossroads and new opportunities.* Washington, DC: Author.

NEW DIRECTIONS FOR YOUTH DEVELOPMENT • DOI: 10.1002/yd

4. Béhague, G. (2006). Diversity and the arts: Issues and strategies. *Latin American Music Review, 27*(1), 26.

5. "We love museums. . . . Do museums love us back?" Retrieved July 9, 2009, from http://www.pinkyshow.org/archives/episodes/081108_museums/.

6. Wheary, J., Shapiro, T. M., Draut, T., & Meschede, T. (2008). *Economic (in)security: The experience of the African American and Latino middle class.* New York and Waltham, MA: Demos and Institute on Assets and Policy at Brandeis University.

7. Wheary et al. (2008).

8. Griffiths, J. M., and King, D.W. (2008, February). Who is visiting museums today? A survey conducted by the Institute for Museum and Library Services. *InterConnections: The IMLS National Study on the Use of Libraries, Museums and the Internet.* Chapel Hill: University of North Carolina claims that 31 percent of Americans visited art museums in 2006. The numbers change when disaggregated by race and educational attainment. Of the Americans who did visit art museums, 36.6 percent were Asian American, 32.2 percent were white, 31.7 percent were Native American, 29.6 percent were "other," and 21 percent were black or African American. Only 5.2 percent of all adult museum goers possessed less than a high school diploma, showing a strong correlation between higher education and museums as recreation.

9. Rockefeller, Jr., D. (1977), *Coming to our senses: The significance of the arts for American education.* New York: McGraw-Hill.

10. National Center for Education Statistics. (2007, September). *Status and trends in the education of racial and ethnic minorities.* Washington, DC: Author.

11. National Endowment for the Arts. (2008). *Artists in the workforce: 1990–2005.* Washington, DC: Office of Research and Analysis.

12. Nusbaum, P. (2004). Folklorists at state arts agencies: Cultural disconnects and "fairness." *Journal of Folklore Research, 41*(2/3), 199–225.

13. Walsh, J. (2004). Pictures, tears, lights, and seats. In J. Cuomo (Ed.), *Whose muse?* Princeton, NJ, and Cambridge, MA: Princeton University Press and Harvard University Press.

14. Cheney, L. (1992). *Telling the truth: A report on the state of the humanities in higher education.* Washington, DC: National Endowment for the Humanities, 1992.

15. Sir Robert Peel, a trustee of the National Gallery quoted in Tyack, G. (1990). "A gallery worthy of the British People": James Pennethorne's designs for the National Gallery, 1845–1867. *Architectural History, 33,* 120–134.

16. Kelley, T. (2003, March–April). Innovation from outside in. *Museum News, 82*(2), 39–61. Retrieved August 30, 2009, from http://www.aam-us.org/pubs/mn/MN_MA03_Inno.

CHRISTINA SUSZYNSKI GREEN *is assistant to the directors of Hospital Audiences and an instructor in the Department of English at the College of New Rochelle's School for New Resources.*

The social power of music can lead to stable and positive changes in individual health and in communities that have significant health risks. Two observers, a medical student and a music student, discuss the ideals and challenges of this principle put into practice.

9

Music as social medicine: Two perspectives on the West-Eastern Divan Orchestra

David M. Washington, Devin G. Beecher

THE WEST-EASTERN DIVAN ORCHESTRA, created in 1999 by Daniel Barenboim and Edward Said, is a brilliantly novel cohort in several senses. The orchestra convenes student musicians, some as young as ten and others in their late twenties, from conflicted Middle Eastern countries to produce a cohesive world-class orchestra. Musicians gain entrance to the Divan through audition and meet each summer near Seville, Spain, to prepare their repertoire for upcoming tours. The music itself, and the students' shared passion for it, provides the foundation for the dynamics, positive and negative, that drive the Divan's social power. We stayed with the orchestra during their training in summer 2008 and have used our observations to reflect on the possibilities of music as a social medicine.

⊕WILEY
InterScience®
DISCOVER SOMETHING GREAT

NEW DIRECTIONS FOR YOUTH DEVELOPMENT, NO. 125, SPRING 2010 © WILEY PERIODICALS, INC.
Published online in Wiley InterScience (www.interscience.wiley.com) • DOI: 10.1002/yd.343

Part One: Two prescriptions from El Sistema and the "West–Eastern Divan Orchestra"

David M. Washington

Western medicine has recently begun to recognize the therapeutic nature of many alternative practices, such as mindfulness and transcendental meditation. Furthering the understanding of these medicines and mechanisms can mean better health for the patient, who expects these stable, inexhaustible, and social sources of health to be efficacious. Of these alternative medicines under scrutiny, music is a known factor.

A brief review of social and public health in war-torn areas

Health, society, and environment have been linked since the days of Socrates.[1] The connection between health and environment as it stands in Western medicine is traced in the work of Rudolf Virchow, *Die Medizinische Reform* [The Medical Reform], where he proposes that individual health is intrinsically linked to the social environment and the policies that shape it. Therefore, social health is also a medical concern. This doctrine is vital to public health and social medicine as practiced in the Western world.[2]

Numerous studies in various fields of medicine have been conducted examining the relationship between concrete socioeconomic disparities and health, as well as the less concrete but real effects of racism on health in the United States.[3] These powerful predictors of health point to disparities and outcomes among populations in American society, such as low birth weights among children born to African American women.[4] Correcting these social inequalities has been a formidable and multifaceted battle.

Some of the tools used to tackle these issues are somewhat unconventional for Western medicine. Using community-based policy reform groups, government-funded community reconstruction, as well as more personal models such as transcendental meditation and mindfulness education, social scientists and doctors have found nonpharmacological but solidly biological means to ameliorate the negative social determinants of health.[5] Stress-coping

NEW DIRECTIONS FOR YOUTH DEVELOPMENT • DOI: 10.1002/yd

resources, mental flexibility, hope, purpose, political empowerment, and education can mitigate the negative power societal stress and disparity have on health.[6] Biologically central in this system is the body's natural stress response, the sympathetic nervous response.[7] The chronic overstimulation of the sympathetic nervous response is associated with many negative health consequences prevalent among the poor and minority populations, such as cardiovascular disease, asthma, violence, and drug-related activity.[8] Triggering this response is stress, scientifically defined as a perceived necessary change in one's current situation without the means to do so.[9] No matter the guise, stress triggers the same biochemical response. Driven by epinephrine and cortisol, stress can contribute to the obesity, heart disease, asthma, and diabetes that are so starkly present in minority communities.[10] Adding stable social assets to communities to combat these stresses or their influences empowers individuals to make healthier choices and support healthy behavior.[11] Music's social influence represents a potent social and biological resource to facilitate better health.[12]

Music as agent of social health

Music has an elaborate history in human civilization. One contemporary example is the way it represents imagined communities of people through national anthems. Music can define generations and groups of individuals, as well as be used for personal therapeutic means by professional music therapists. It stands to reason that music should be explored in its capacity to promote healing and health in a larger context. There have been several initiatives in North, Central, and South America, and more broadly in the scope of international experiences, that pursue this health-enhancing effect of music. One of the most successful is known as El sistema, developed by José Abreu in underserved communities throughout Venezuela.

Thirty years ago, working under the conviction that "music begets human harmony," Abreu and his associates developed a national infrastructure that supports youth orchestras in every city and produces the concrete product of a concert. Central to this movement is the idea of *tocar y luchar*, which translates as "to play and to struggle." Abreu expounds on this, saying that one must struggle for what one wants, even when the goal is music.[13]

For the sake of young people in Venezuela who otherwise would have few outlets for their talents and their hopes, Abreu dedicates his work to multiplying sites of classical music. He creates communities that have the "fundamental objective" of achieving the mission of creating orchestras.[14] Indeed, those who organize and participate in the orchestra give moving testimonies to the effect that they become "part of a family." The communication and unity the orchestras construct in this program serve not only to benefit the participants, but also the general communities in which they practice and perform.[15] Indeed the sociological structure of the country is altered as the government and the people it represents are intertwined with the youth orchestras on both a patriotic level and a fiscal one. The program supports three to four orchestras in each nucleus of every state in Venezuela.

A significant aspect of the program that enhances its power to educate and to unify is the extent of its youth involvement.[16] Incorporating children as young as two years old to those in their twenties, the program involves approximately 240,000 Venezuelan youths.[17] Through the discipline and self-perpetuating good habits that music practice imparts, the lives of the young musicians develop along these healthy principles. Conductor Simón Rattle explains that art strives for perfection. Its pursuit requires excellence, order, hard work, and determination. Music education thus empowers the pursuit of perfection, and "your life goes with your instrument."[18] Instead of feeling forced to turn to drugs or violence in a society of limited resources and social mobility, young people recognize the option of music, the support of the community, and the irrevocable personal and interpersonal education attained through participation in the orchestra.

Education correlates with better social and personal health.[19] In this sense, music is a social asset and cofactor of good health, as it provides social values and public works that not only enrich lives but also save lives. The proof of its positive results is in the organization's participants, many of whom practice vigorously on their own time, striving to be ever better musicians. One of the young musicians literally sleeps with his cello.[20] Even blind and deaf youth are involved in this cultural phenomenon, performing a mixed dance/choral-like art as a way to interpret music.[21] This integrates and connects them to their peers and the community, providing purpose, hope, and education that permeate society, so that music becomes an efficacious agent of social health.[22]

A case study in an Arab-Israeli community

Another example of music's therapeutic effects is the West-Eastern Divan Orchestra. Founded in 1999 by Argentinean-Israeli conductor Daniel Barenboim and Palestinian-American literary scholar and public intellectual Edward Said, the group breaks down ignorance and hate among the cultures of the Middle East.[23] They gathered some of the finest young musicians from Egypt, Iran, Syria, Palestine, Jordan, and Lebanon, cultures that otherwise have little to no civic interaction, and fostered cooperation and collaboration through musical practice and performance. As one member of the orchestra eloquently puts it, the orchestra enables our "playing in harmony."[24] The need for such social change is critically tied to the health of the Middle East, as the chronic stress of warfare and hatred has certainly taken its toll.[25]

Many have documented the significant psychosocial effects of war in the psychological pathology of civilian populations of war-torn areas. Most agree that permanent healing in this region can occur only with the institution of social structures that provide a stable source of positive and novel interaction; that is, peace depends on activities that can construct society rather than destroy it.[26] The Divan Orchestra does just that. The program lays a foundation in productive collaboration in music and then, as a corollary, creates a safe forum for discussion of the issues plaguing the Middle East. The dialogue encouraged in the discussions continues beyond this forum into the musicians' leisure time, whether at the local *cervezeria* or in the halls of the dormitory. In this dynamic inside and outside the orchestra, the members of conflicted communities are empowered to challenge their own understanding of their situation, and perhaps to change their perceived positions.[27] With the realization that an "enemy" is much like oneself comes a new understanding and valuation of human life—one that may serve to undercut the prejudice and hatred propagated through war. Many of the members in the group felt this way.[28]

In the discussions and relationships created in music, some gained hope for the future and felt that collaborative efforts could be extended even beyond this program. In essence, a new, supportive society is traced out for the future of the Middle East. Such a movement may pale in comparison to obstacles that decades of war have burgeoned; however, it is a beginning and an entity from which growth can occur, just as boycotts in Montgomery, Alabama, were a beginning to some of the biggest social changes America has ever seen.

Many of the members of the group who had participated in this program felt that the social movement developing in the Divan Orchestra extended to the communities they played for and also to their home nations. As one member put it, "Wherever we go, we are ambassadors of hope and peace."[29] Every movement, especially community-based public health initiatives, requires ambassadors. The musicians of the Divan represent how music can be a viable amenity to this end for those in health care.

Part Two: Perspectives on knowledge, from the Divan Orchestra and Providence Community MusicWorks

Devin G. Beecher

Paul Smaczny's 2005 documentary of the Divan Orchestra, *Knowledge Is the Beginning*, takes its title from a phrase uttered by Daniel Barenboim in the film's second scene.[1] Barenboim sits in the passenger seat of a car driving through Ramallah; checkpoint after checkpoint turn what should be a short ride into a day's journey as he and Mustafa Barghouthi, from the Palestinian National Initiative, discuss the appalling ignorance of both Israelis and Palestinians of their respective situations. "Because knowledge is the beginning," proposes Barenboim. "I think the only hope is that contacts are created with people on both sides who are unhappy with the way things are now and the way things are going, and try and find a common ground."

I supposed that a probable beginning location for this knowledge was at the orchestra's annual retreat in Pilas, Spain, the final week of which David Washington and I were lucky enough to be invited to attend. My hopes were high: It is hard not to have high hopes after seeing the Divan Orchestra live, as I had two years before when they visited Providence, Rhode Island. During their three-day residency at Brown University, I witnessed a number of hopeful things: the obvious friendships among its members, the preeminent musical leadership of Daniel Barenboim, the unity of musical idea shared by the orchestra, and the conviction with which they presented it. Optimism unfurls with the Divan Orchestra's inspiring performances: playing in harmony and with musical unity signifies the potential for living in harmony and with political unity in the Middle East.

Musical knowledges

In Pilas, I was to hear almost nothing about the conflict during the following week, though it was in search of this sort of knowledge that I had come. The knowledge I found instead was almost entirely musical. It began even before the first tutti rehearsal with Barenboim the next afternoon. The schedule that morning was individual instrument sectionals, and, being a horn player, I snuck into horn sectionals and introduced myself to the coach. One of the players was sick that day, and as I just happened to have brought my horn along, I found myself subbing for him on the second horn part of the Schönberg Variations for Orchestra. I learned in the space of an hour who had solid intonation, who had rhythmic difficulties, who had trouble articulating piano passages, who had learned their part and who had not. I became acquainted with each of the player's tones in all dynamic ranges, and after the rehearsal I figured out what types of horns they played and with whom they had studied.

NEW DIRECTIONS FOR YOUTH DEVELOPMENT • DOI: 10.1002/yd

What I acquired in these two hours was a very interpersonal sort of knowledge that comes from making music with other people— even if I still knew little about these players' histories and personalities, I now knew very well their playing styles, their strengths, and their weaknesses. This may in fact be one of the most concrete knowledges developed by the Divan Orchestra in their intensive workshop in Pilas and in the tours that follow. This is evident throughout Smaczny's documentary, especially in an interview between the two concertmasters, Claude, from Lebanon, and Ilya, from Israel. Claude says, "The first two days it was funny, people are playing different, but now they are like a team, now they are playing together, now they understand more. . . . Now I know how he plays and he knows how the way I am. So we actually have some connection when we're out on the same stand." This is the inevitable result of playing together, and it is the beginning of a knowledge that should not be dismissed.

There was also the more purely musical knowledge imparted by Barenboim during the long, intense, and efficient daily rehearsals. My notebook is filled with underlined exclamatory notations: "Taking time is the last resort to musicality!" "Always play against maximum resistance, not minimum resistance!" "Sound diminishes naturally, so whenever we sustain sound, we create tension!" I sat with the horn section during one rehearsal in order to watch Barenboim's conducting more carefully. He seems to sing with his arms, and even if he were to make not a single comment for an entire rehearsal, one could still learn from his expressive gestures. The orchestra absorbs his musicality as much as they can: this is evident in the rapt attention they pay him during rehearsals and the familiarity with the music and unity of playing they evince during performances.

The only official discussion that took place this week of the workshop was also focused entirely on music—on opera, in particular, a genre that many of the students were formerly unfamiliar with. Michael Steinberg, professor of music at Brown University and director of Brown University's Cogut Center for the Humanities, moderated a discussion between Daniel Barenboim and Patrice

Chereau. The orchestra was to play the entire first act of *Die Walküre* on tour, and so after an afternoon rehearsal, there was a screening of this act from Chereau's famous 1976 production of the Ring Cycle for the centennial of the Bayreuth Festspeilhaus. The production was a complete scandal, primarily because, as Steinberg put it, "the real world is on stage in Bayreuth." The very conservative audience did not expect "that a language of emotion and myth would be interrupted by a visual as well as dramatic language of history and reality." This act in particular had caused an uproar due to its foregrounding of incest, which previous directors had attempted to hide: the curtain closes as Siegmund and Sieglinde, son and daughter of Wotan, mount each other on the ground.

Dinner followed the screening, and discussion followed the dinner. Michael Steinberg opened the discussion, though most direction thereafter came from the students in the orchestra. Topics included the relation between the stage acting and the music, and in particular how Chereau dealt with Wagner's use of character leitmotifs. Chereau and Barenboim also discussed the collaboration between conductor and stage director. Often Barenboim would detour from the discussion to give the orchestra explanations of things he expected they might not know: for instance, how most opera productions are prepared. "I don't understand colleagues who conduct opera and are not interested in the theatrical aspect of it," complained Barenboim, contrasting typical opera production processes which entail a disconnect between preparation of the orchestra and stage, with his and Chereau's more collaborative approach. For aspiring musicians with little operatic experience or knowledge, a discussion with such an eminent conductor, director, and scholar was a fantastic beginning.

A question that never came up, however—and if it was because Barenboim has already dealt with it so much in his past, this denies its continuing controversial nature—was what Barenboim and the Israeli 30 percent of the orchestra were doing performing Wagner in the first place. Barenboim had touched on the issue gracefully a few days before in rehearsal, when he mentioned that Wagner had accused Jews of being poor musicians because of the up-and-down nature of synagogue music—they were thus unable to sustain a musical line. Barenboim dismissed the absurdity of this accusation by not dealing with it, instead emphasizing Wagner's artistic argument and urging his orchestra to think of music as moving horizontally rather than vertically. In the Wagner discussion, though, they did not even come this close to the minefield of opinions surrounding Wagner, and what I had expected to be a controversial and exciting night was merely stimulating and informative. I reflected that the entire week had been this way as well.

Experiencing the mission

In my week in Pilas, I had discovered a wealth of musical knowledge, and doubtless the students participating in the workshop had learned even more. However, was this knowledge the sort that Barenboim had hoped for to begin with? Could political enlightenment follow from musical enlightenment? In Smaczny's documentary, Bassam, a student from Syria, extols to the camera "the idea of just getting together these people from different countries from the Middle East . . . sharing music stands together, playing music, playing in harmony, so to speak. . . . Through that common ground or common interest there is, I think, a good chance for us to get into other topics and other ideas that we might not agree on, but at least we have a chance for dialogue."[2]

There was, as far as I could tell, no such dialogue. No organized political discussion took place while Barenboim was in Pilas, and according to a woman I talked to who worked at one of the foundation's schools in Ramallah, the discussions that occurred before Barenboim's (and my) arrival were heated but unproductive: students voiced their opinions without listening to anybody else speak. In the late evenings, groups of students dotted the beautiful grounds, but walking through this picturesque scene, I rarely heard any English being spoken. Because English is a required common language in the orchestra, this would have been a sign of potentially productive conversations going on between students from different parts of the world. After hours of grueling rehearsal, of course, it was understandable that students would rather speak their native language with people from their own part of the world. However, it seemed that the acquisition of so much musical knowledge in one day became a hindrance rather than a beginning to further discussion of more problematic topics during these evenings.

There were, of course, the table tennis matches, the trips to bars nearby, the pool party on the last night, and other social activities that many members of the orchestra took part in. These were often wider in scope, bringing together students from all parts of the Middle East and elsewhere in the world. Certainly musical as well as social interaction is better than no interaction, and the fact that each student recognized through these activities their shared traits, interests, and humanity is indeed hopeful and probably beneficial. However, it did not seem that meaningful knowledge or contrasting perspectives were shared and discussed in these situations. Perhaps it is too much to expect for a student orchestra, working so hard during the day, to find the time, energy, or curiosity to have discussions of this sort.

Troubled by this, on returning to the United States I contacted Community MusicWorks, an organization in Providence, Rhode Island, with similar ideas of the social change that music can effect. Sebastian Ruth founded this group in 1997 and is currently its executive-artistic director, as well as the violist in the Providence String Quartet, whose permanent residency is at the organization's core. Ruth was highly involved with the Divan Orchestra's 2006 visit to Providence in which the Providence quartet collaborated with Divan's front-stand players to perform Mendelssohn's String Octet in open rehearsal with Daniel Barenboim. When I expressed my concern to Ruth about the lack of the political discussions I had hoped to witness in Pilas, he responded: "You don't need to talk about the 'mission' in order to experience the mission." Just as Barenboim has insisted that the Divan Orchestra is a musical, not a political, endeavor, so did Ruth describe Community MusicWorks as "first and foremost about music." My reservations, it now seemed, were based on my expectations that the Divan Orchestra be more than it is. In my week in Pilas, I witnessed the accumulation of precious musical knowledge and also real social connections.

NEW DIRECTIONS FOR YOUTH DEVELOPMENT • DOI: 10.1002/yd

Did these necessarily further political understanding? Ruth was wise on this question as well: He proposed that the Divan Orchestra is an "opportunity for people to have an experience that builds trust with someone from the opposite side of the conflict," but as for the effects of this trust, "you can't measure that for a long time." Knowledge is the beginning.

The danger is that the Divan Orchestra's concerts seem anything but a beginning. Watching the harmonious way the orchestra performs and interacts, one expects that the members would be more than musicians: perhaps an army of politically enlightened citizens bound to positively influence the future of the Middle East. That indeed was my high hope en route to Pilas. They are not this; instead, they are fantastic musicians who are able to make fantastic music with people who otherwise and elsewhere would be their enemies. Their unity of musical feeling should not be seen as a metaphor for unity in the Middle East. Viewing it this way is potentially counterproductive: if audiences, particularly elite Europe audiences, see it as a vastly hopeful sign that progress toward unity and healing is being made by the project, they may thus adopt a more complacent attitude toward the conflict in the Middle East. The Divan Orchestra should be viewed instead as the end product, artificially sustained through the musical brilliance of Daniel Barenboim, of a causal relationship whose antecedent is still utterly lacking. If progress toward peace is made in the Middle East, then this beautiful music and much more could be the result.

Notes for Part One

1. Public Health. (2008). *Encyclopædia Britannica Online*. Retrieved August 22, 2008, from http://www.britannica.com/EBchecked/topic/482384/public-health.

2. Ritchie, D. (2008). *What is health equity?* In SNMA Black History Month Noontime Lecture 2008. Providence, RI: BioMedical Center of Brown University; Rudolf Virchow. (2009). Encyclopaedia Britannica Online. Retrieved January 17, 2008, from http://www.britannica.com/EBchecked/topic/629797/Rudolf-Carl-Virchow/7718/Early-career.

3. *Unnatural Causes: Is inequality making us sick?* (Series). California Newsreel with Vital Pictures [DVD]. San Francisco: National Minority Consortia,

2008; Britton, W. (2004). *The pathophysiology of stress and depression.* Providence, RI: Brown University Medical School.

4. Arvelo, A. (2006). *Tocar Y Luchar.* Caracas, Venezuela: Cinema Sur, Explorart Films.

5. Ritchie. (2008). Davis, J. M., & Baker, B. T. (2007). A pilot study on mindfulness based stress reduction for smokers. *BMC Complementary and Alternative Medicine (online),* 7(2), 1–7; Schneider, R. H., Alexander, C. N., Staggers, F., Orme-Johnson, D. W., Rainforth, M., Salerno, J. W., et al. (2005). A randomized controlled trial of stress reduction in African Americans treated for hypertension for over one year. *American Journal of Hypertension, 18*(1), 88–98.

6. Britton. (2004).

7. Britton. (2004).

8. *Unnatural causes: Is inequality making us sick?* (2008); Britton. (2004); Cengage. (2001).

9. Britton. (2004).

10. *Unnatural causes: Is inequality making us sick?* (2008); Ritchie. (2008).

11. *Unnatural causes: Is inequality making us sick?* (2008); Cengage. (2001); Ritchie. (2008).

12. Boso, M., Politi, P., Barale, F., and Emanuele, E. (2006). Neurophysiology and neurobiology of the musical experience. *Functional Neurology, 21*(4), 187–191; Cash, A. (2008). *Music and stress management.* Retrieved June 10, 2008, from http://www.healingmusicenterprises.com/articles/music_stress_management.html.

13. Arvelo. (2006).

14. Arvelo. (2006).

15. Arvelo. (2006).

16. Arvelo. (2006).

17. Arvelo. (2006).

18. Arvelo. (2006).

19. *Unnatural causes: Is inequality making us sick?* (2008); Ritchie. (2008).

20. Arvelo. (2006).

21. Arvelo. (2006).

22. Public Health. (2008); Britton. (2004); Wallerstein, N. (2002). Empowerment to reduce health disparities. *Scandinavian Journal of Public Health, 30*(3), 72–77.

23. Heller, A. (2005). *Knowledge is the beginning: Daniel Barenboim and the West-Eastern Divan Orchestra.* New York: Warner.

24. Heller. (2005).

25. Skinner, H., Abdeen, Z., Aber, P., Al-Masri, M., Attias, J., Avraham, K. B., et al. (2005). Promoting Arab and Israeli cooperation: Peacebuilding through health initiatives. *Lancet, 365,* 1274–1277; Summerfield, D. (2000). War and mental health: A brief overview. *British Medical Journal, 321,* 232–235; Tobin, J. P. (2000). Observations on the mental health of civilian populations living under long-term hostilities. *Psychiatric Bulletin, 24,* 69–70.

26. Dajani, K. K., & Carel, R. S. (2002). Neighbors and enemies: Lessons to be learned from the Palestinian-Israeli conflict regarding cooperation and

public health. *Croatian Medical Journal, 43*(2), 138–140; Skiller et al. (2005); Summerfield. (2000).

27. Washington, D. (2008). *Music as medicine.* Providence, RI: Warren Alpert Medical School of Brown University.

28. Washington. (2008).

29. Washington. (2008).

Notes for Part Two

1. Smaczny, P. (2006). *Knowledge is the beginning* [DVD]. EuroArts Music International GmbH, 2006 (90 min.)

2. Smaczny. (2006).

DAVID M. WASHINGTON *is a third-year medical student at the Warren Alpert Medical School of Brown University.*

DEVIN G. BEECHER *is pursuing a career as a French horn player.*

This article examines Forum Theater and critical literacy with immigrants in an English class and identifies the revolutionary and pedagogical possibilities of a theater where there are only spectactors.

10

Boal's Theater of the Oppressed and how to derail real-life tragedies with imagination

Maria Tereza Schaedler

THE MEANING OF THEATER in the process of transmitting knowledge has been extensively debated throughout the history of humanity. From Aristotle to Boal, theater has been discussed as art for contemplation and art for transformation. Based on several articles about drama in education, it sounds as if there is a stereotypical view that views theater as being only a performance on stage. This simplistic way to look at theater seems to be one of the reasons for the resistance in using drama in the classroom. There is an expectation that children have to perform a play for an audience instead of just benefiting from drama as a process of make-believe.[1]

Not all educators feel comfortable directing and staging plays, but it does not have to be like that. As Andersen said, "In a staged theater production, there is often more of a focus on rehearsal as a means to a end (that end being the performance). In drama in

education, the process is the end in itself."[2] What educators need to understand is that it is not about the performance at the end, but the process of using drama, the techniques and exercises, that can open up a world of possibilities in the classroom. Of course, it can have a final product and it can be a performance, but this is not necessary to develop this work.

Theater of the Oppressed

As an artist and an educator, I always felt comfortable using drama techniques. After training with Brazilian theater director Augusto Boal, I decided to study and apply his own techniques known as Theater of the Oppressed (TO), which focuses on the process. Every human being is theater, and theater is necessarily political. This is how Boal conceived TO over thirty years ago. The extensive literature involving TO, authored by Boal and others, shows how widely practiced it is in many countries. Boal states that the TO has two fundamental principles: "1) To help the spectator become a protagonist of the dramatic action so that s/he can 2) apply those actions s/he has practiced in the theater to real life."[3] One of Boal's most translated books is *Theater of the Oppressed*, where he explores the social constructs that lie behind the traditional theater form while analyzing Aristotle, Machiavelli, Hegel, and Brecht.[4]

Boal created the TO in Brazil with the goal of dealing with social and political problems inside communities. He uses theater as the language to speak about all kinds of human concerns and social issues. Some of its major techniques are Image Theater, Forum Theater, Cops in the Head, and Rainbow of Desire.

The techniques

In Image Theater, participants use the bodies of the other participants to sculpt their opinions and feelings. Boal believes that this form has the "extraordinary capacity for making thought *visible*."[5] Images are a language like any other, with its collective denotations and individual connotations. Boal affirmed that "oppression exists when a dialogue becomes a monologue."[6] When one side tries to dominate the other, the dialogue turns into a monologue. "Images convey ideas";[7] therefore Image Theater can be a powerful tool to create dialogue.

Forum Theater is identified as a problem-solving technique. A story of oppression is improvised, and the public is invited to stop the action, replace the character that is being oppressed, and improvise a new ending. For Boal, "Often a person is very revolutionary when in a public forum he envisages and advocates revolutionary and heroic acts; on the other hand, he often realizes that things are not so easy when he himself has to practice what he suggests."[8] Forum Theater can be used to look at past and present situations, or it can be a rehearsal for the future.

Cops in the Head is an element of a broader concept inside the structure of TO. This method is concerned with individuals' internal voices, fears, and oppressions. "To know and to transform" is the goal of this technique that helps to bring to light the "cops" inside one's head.[9] Rainbow of Desire is a more complex technique. It is a process of exploring the "rainbow" of fears and desires of each character. This technique uses Image Theater to bring to life conflicting emotions and deconstructs the character's story of conflict.

Boal insists that the spectator must become the *spect-actor.* He or she becomes the protagonist of the story, "changes the dramatic action, tries out solutions, discusses plans for change—in short, trains him[her]self for the real action. In this case, perhaps the theater is not revolutionary in itself, but it is surely a rehearsal for the revolution."[10] This is an important concept for TO, and it creates an opportunity for people to identify commonalities and learn about the differences between individuals.

The study

For two months I conducted a pilot study involving Brazilian immigrants in a class for English for speakers of other languages (ESOL). The study consisted of using Forum Theater techniques as a pedagogical tool to help these students develop critical literacy skills in English. Some of the findings of this study are that this technique improves participants' social awareness, transforms people into protagonists of their own lives, and helps develop language skills.

The setting of the study was an ESOL class for immigrants held in Everett, Massachusetts, a working-class suburb of Boston. This study was conducted with adults, but the same techniques can and have been applied with a group of young immigrants. This class was an academic year-long program for local residents, and it was considered at an intermediate/advanced level. Research was conducted over a two-month period, with seven class sessions, each extending over two and a half hours. Data were gathered and analyzed while exploring participants' reactions through interviews, group discussions, and observations.

The research intervention for this study was the application of Forum Theater to the curriculum. The Forum Theater process started by creating a safe environment with warm-ups and improvisational theater games for people to share personal stories. In the next step, participants chose one of the stories (the one that they related most with) to intervene. One of the stories was about two people disguised as police officers who threatened and robbed immigrants. The improvisation of the story followed, and spect-actors started imagining what they could do to change the outcome of the story. The spect-actor took on the role of the protagonist and improvised a new ending to the story instead of just sharing verbally what the protagonist should or could do. While advocating for themselves and for each other in the story, they all became emotional and angry.

In this study, I found that no matter why the participants were studying English, the reasons were all rooted in becoming autonomous in society. Speaking English can give immigrants confidence to communicate and interact in any social context, and it can play an important role for the adaptation process of immigrant youth. Data from this study indicate that the participants' experiences speaking English are often embedded in fear. They often noted that they are afraid of making mistakes and being laughed at.

Improving their language skills gave the participants confidence and self-esteem, as well as better chances of advocating for themselves. In interviews, they said that the use of theater techniques helped them feel more relaxed, and that contributed to the development of their self-esteem in their adaptation process. To speak English is more than a survival skill for immigrant families; it helps both adults and children act as protagonists of their lives. Theater of the Oppressed empowers immigrants who are learning a new language by giving them the opportunity to rehearse their language skills in situations that are going to be relevant for them.

An interesting phenomenon reported by immigrants in this study is the new relationship established between adults and youth in the new culture. Parents reported that they became much more dependent on their children, who were able to conquer the language barrier much more quickly. As children developed a new sense of responsibility in the family as communicators and translators, parents had to give up some control, reversing the role of parents and children, which can be very stressful for the family.

Adults in this study reported that among the reasons they needed to improve their English skills was to help their children with homework. Practicing English through theater was more than a possible avenue to develop this goal. It was also a way of developing confidence and self-esteem.

The connection with critical literacy

Paulo Freire, the Brazilian educator who became known worldwide for *Pedagogy of the Oppressed*, believed that language is culture; by learning how to use language, people recognize themselves as the subject of the history process and therefore can change their realities.[11] Because immigrant children learn how to use the new language faster than adults, their adaptation in the new culture is smoother than that of their parents, which does not mean that it is an easy process.

Giroux notes in the introduction of Freire and Macedo's book *Literacy: Reading the Word and the World* that teachers need to introduce a language of empowerment to students.[12] This language is critical literacy, and it allows students to think and reflect about their lives before they can take actions. This language of empowerment reconstructs people's social understanding, helping them to take risks to transform themselves and envision a new world.

Developing critical literacy and finding a voice in another language had an impact on the participants' cultural identities. The participants were transformed into what Freire called "conscious beings."[13] The majority of immigrants in the United States represent what Freire would call a dependent, silent society: "Its voice is not an authentic voice, but merely an echo of the voice of the metropolis—in every way, the metropolis speaks, the dependent society listens."[14] What is needed in this case is a "revolutionary project . . . a process in which the people assume the role of subject in the precarious adventure of transforming and recreating the world."[15] Conscious beings question their cultural identities and decide what they should keep, what needs to be transformed, and what they want to acquire. They become subjects in every context.

The process of becoming a conscious being is not easy and has some costs. I realized how much I was asking of the participants in this study. I wanted them to run over their fears, take risks, and engage in improvisational theater techniques. I asked them not only to use the new language they were learning, but their bodies as well. I put them in a very vulnerable position. Even so, during a particular Forum Theater session, everybody in the class participated. One by one, they were assuming the role of protagonist and changing the outcome of the story. Some of them demonstrated a certain ease and confidence. Others were timid at the start, but they were encouraged by the rest of the group, and by the end, they were not only more self-assured but also had smiles on their faces.

In this situation, I found an important connection between improving language skills and empowerment. The connection was made when the spect-actors forgot they were in an English class

NEW DIRECTIONS FOR YOUTH DEVELOPMENT • DOI: 10.1002/yd

and eventually even forgot they were speaking English. They were actively engaged in their roles, and that was because the story was relevant to them.

Results

I could not measure the efficacy of this technique outside the classroom. However, I discovered how the simple action of engaging in a dialogue could be empowering. Being able to communicate, share ideas, and agree or disagree is not a simple task when people do not share the same language and culture. Theater of the Oppressed can stimulate dialogue and is useful to develop critical literacy in the classroom because it has reflective and transformative possibilities. TO helps develop spoken and nonverbal dialogue through a personalization of the learning process. New ideas are constructed through students' stories. TO can also be a powerful tool to analyze the relationship between immigrant parents and children. Having both groups represented at a Forum Theater session could potentially illuminate the complexity of this relationship and help to transform it.

As a pedagogical strategy, Forum Theater demonstrated itself to be useful in developing communication skills in an ESOL environment. Participants in this course placed great value on developing their oral language skills. The fact that students became subjects and challenged the power structure in the classroom using this technique helped them develop critical literacy. Theater of the Oppressed is not a magical tool and will not solve all problems. It is a process that helps people become aware of the problems so they can analyze them and try to identify possible solutions.

As Freire stated, "There is no way to transformation, transformation is the way."[16] If what we are looking for is transformation, then we have to start transforming the world around us. In order to transform their realities, immigrants have to shift from being an object to becoming a subject. Although I could not measure how the participants were using their skills outside the classroom, I still believe that this work gave them the awareness of possibilities for action. In these experiences with Forum Theater, I discovered they can become their own advocates. Participants learned that they could rely on themselves. In this study, some participants were nervous about standing up and speaking English in the Forum Theater sessions, but they did it nevertheless, and they became agents in the classroom.

During this study, I also realized that although Theater of the Oppressed is an excellent tool to develop critical consciousness, this theater in ESOL classes needs to recognize the goals of this setting—in this case, language acquisition. In the study, by becoming conscious beings, participants were also able to learn English.

I never had the audacity to think that I could empower the students myself. I could only offer them a tool and hope that they would choose to use it. And they did. Some of the participants are now becoming facilitators of Forum Theater activities in lower-level English classes in the same program, and three of them are now officially teaching English. Forum Theater helped them to figure out what to do with this new voice in this new culture. It is a new identity they created, which added to the other identities they already had.[17] By disseminating this technique and helping other immigrants develop their language skills, subjects from this study are now developing their own powers to transform and become agents of change.

Learning and final considerations regarding youth

This work can be applied in any context. It is a powerful tool to be used with children and parents. By using drama in education, we are giving young people and adults the opportunity to diversify their knowledge and create an atmosphere where they can free their potentialities and express feelings, emotions, and anxieties. When a student interprets a character or dramatizes a situation, he or she is revealing a part of himself or herself. By using drama, they show how they see, feel, and think in the world. Boal believed that "if the person has changed, something has changed around. If you acquire knowledge of something, this knowledge changes you and you change people around you."[18]

Theater of the Oppressed techniques can be used to show young people that they can be agents of their own lives. Through scenes and dialogues, they realize that they have their own voice and are able to change their surroundings. For immigrant youth specifically, it can help them understand their new role in the family. When working with youth, improvised role play, and conflicts, it is important to emphasize that they should not try to find a magical solution or use violence to solve the problem. Theater of the Oppressed is based on nonviolent efforts to change a situation and can be helpful with groups of youth challenged by violence in their lives.

Theater stimulates dialogue and creates critical consciousness. It is a nonviolent approach to problem solving, shows people that there is not only one frame of reference in the world, challenges traditional power roles in the classroom, stimulates imagination and creativity, and strikes people in a unique way that a lecture will likely not.

This is a powerful tool to develop critical literacy. Theater of the Oppressed and critical literacy have the same goal. So the question is, "How many classes are doing TO?" Not many. Why? What do we need to do to use more TO in this context? And how are we going to do this? My guess is that many classes do not use TO because they are not familiar with this approach or are afraid to use it. Teachers are also products of banking education and are afraid of giving up power; it is too risky for them. They often do not want to lose control and allow the unexpected to happen.

For those seeking to develop this work, I recommend flexibility and full commitment during the entire process. The teacher-facilitator must determine his or her own training. I advise becoming very familiar with TO techniques before applying them in the classroom. The more the facilitator is knowledgeable about all TO procedures, the better he or she will be at adapting the techniques to the needs of students. I encourage teachers, facilitators, researchers, and instructors to take risks, and I invite students to take risks as well. I recommend everybody to honestly engage in a learning process with other people and be open to learning from failures and mistakes. And again, keep in mind Freire's message: "There is no way to transformation, transformation is the way."[19]

As a theater practitioner, I am a witness of the power of arts and the positive changes it can bring. "If you have a strong desire, if you have not given up and you still believe, things can be changed."[20] Even if you change only yourself, I believe this work is worth it, because when we change, people around us change as well. The awareness that drama can build up new knowledge for children is where all educators should start.

Notes

1. Blatner, A. (Ed.), with Wiener, D. J. (2007). Applications in education. In *Interactive and improvisational drama: Varieties of applied theater and performance*. New York: iUniverse.

2. Andersen, C. (2004). Learning in "as if" worlds: Cognition in drama in education. *Theory into Practice, 43*(4), 281–286. P. 282.

3. Boal, A. (1990). The cop in the head. Three hypotheses. *Drama Review, 34*(3), 35–42. P. 36.

4. Boal, A. (1985). *Theater of the oppressed.* New York: Theater Communication Group.

5. Boal. (1985). P. 137.

6. Boal. (1990). P. 47.

7. Boal. (1990). P. 48.

8. Boal. (1985). P. 139.

9. Boal, A. (2004). *Games for actors and non-actors.* New York: Routledge. P. 207.

10. Boal. (1990). P. 122.

11. Freire, P. (2007). *Pedagogy of the oppressed.* New York: Continuum.

12. Giroux, H. (1987). Literacy and the pedagogy of political empowerment. In P. Freire & D. Macedo (Eds.), *Literacy: Reading the word and the world.* Westport, CT: Bergin & Garvey.

13. Freire, P. (2000). Cultural action for freedom. *Harvard Educational Review.* Monograph Series, No. 1. P. 39.

14. Freire. (2000). P. 46.

15. Freire. (2000). P. 56.

16. Freire, P., & Macedo, D. (1987). *Literacy: Reading the word and the world.* Westport, CT: Bergin & Garvey. P. 7.

17. Schaedler, M. (2008). *"Transformation is the way": A study about Forum Theater and critical literacy with Brazilian immigrants in an ESOL class in New England.* Unpublished master's thesis, Lesley University.

18. Boal, A. (1996). *Politics, education and change. Drama, culture and empowerment.* Brisbane, Australia: IDEA Publications. P. 50.

19. Freire & Macedo. (1987). P. 7.

20. Paterson, D., & Weinberg, M. (1996). We are all theater: An interview with Augusto Boal. *High Performance Magazine.* Retrieved September 19, 2007, from http://www.communityarts.net/readingroom/archivefiles/2002/09/we_all_are_thea.php.

MARIA TEREZA SCHAEDLER *is a Brazilian artist and educator.*

Index

153

Notes for Conributors

After reading this issue, you might be interested in becoming a contributor to *New Directions for Youth Development: Theory, Practice, and Research*. In the tradition of the New Directions series, each volume of the journal addresses a single, timely topic, although special issues covering a variety of topics are occasionally commissioned. Submissions should address the implications of theory for practice and research directions, and how these arenas can better inform one another. Articles may focus on any aspect of youth development; all theoretical and methodological orientations are welcome.

If you would like to serve as an issue editor, you can email the editor-in-chief, Gil Noam, at Gil_Noam@harvard.edu. If he approves of your idea, the next step would be to submit an outline of no more than three pages that includes a brief description of your proposed topic and its significance, along with a brief synopsis of individual articles (including tentative authors and a working title for each chapter).

If you are interested in contributing an individual article, please contact the managing editor Erin Cooney at ecooney@mclean .harvard.edu first to see whether the topic will fit with any of the upcoming issues. The upcoming issues are listed on our Web site, www.pearweb.org/ndyd. If the article does fit topically, the managing editor will send you guidelines for submission.

For all prospective issue editors:

- Please make sure to keep accessibility in mind, by illustrating theoretical ideas with specific examples and explaining technical terms in nontechnical language. A busy practitioner who may not have an extensive research background should be well served by our work.

- Please keep in mind that references should be limited to twenty-five to thirty per article. Authors should make use of case examples to illustrate their ideas, rather than citing exhaustive research references. For readers who want to delve more deeply into a particular topic, you and/or chapter authors may want to recommend two or three key articles, books, or Web sites that are influential in the field, to be featured on a resource page.
- All reference information should be listed as endnotes, rather than including author names in the body of the article or footnotes at the bottom of the page. The endnotes are in APA style.
- Please visit http://www.pearweb.org for more information.

Gil G. Noam
Editor-in-Chief

ORDER FORM SUBSCRIPTION AND SINGLE ISSUES

DISCOUNTED BACK ISSUES:

Use this form to receive 20% off all back issues of *New Directions for Youth Development*.
All single issues priced at **$23.20** (normally $29.00)

TITLE   ISSUE NO.   ISBN

_____   _____   _____

_____   _____   _____

_____   _____   _____

Call 888-378-2537 or see mailing instructions below. When calling, mention the promotional code JB9ND
to receive your discount. For a complete list of issues, please visit www.josseybass.com/go/ndyd

SUBSCRIPTIONS: (1 YEAR, 4 ISSUES)

☐ New Order   ☐ Renewal

U.S.	☐ Individual: $85	☐ Institutional: $228
CANADA/MEXICO	☐ Individual: $85	☐ Institutional: $268
ALL OTHERS	☐ Individual: $109	☐ Institutional: $302

Call 888-378-2537 or see mailing and pricing instructions below.
Online subscriptions are available at www.interscience.wiley.com

ORDER TOTALS:

Issue / Subscription Amount: $ _____

Shipping Amount: $ _____
(for single issues only – subscription prices include shipping)

Total Amount: $ _____

SHIPPING CHARGES:	
First Item	$5.00
Each Add'l Item	$3.00

(No sales tax for U.S. subscriptions. Canadian residents, add GST for subscription orders. Individual rate subscriptions must
be paid by personal check or credit card. Individual rate subscriptions may not be resold as library copies.)

BILLING & SHIPPING INFORMATION:

☐ **PAYMENT ENCLOSED:** *(U.S. check or money order only. All payments must be in U.S. dollars.)*

☐ **CREDIT CARD:**   ☐ VISA   ☐ MC   ☐ AMEX

Card number _____ Exp. Date _____

Card Holder Name_____ Card Issue # _____

Signature _____ Day Phone _____

☐ **BILL ME:** *(U.S. institutional orders only. Purchase order required.)*

Purchase order # _____
Federal Tax ID 13559302 • GST 89102-8052

Name _____

Address_____

Phone_____ E-mail_____

Copy or detach page and send to: **John Wiley & Sons, PTSC, 5th Floor**
989 Market Street, San Francisco, CA 94103-1741

Order Form can also be faxed to: **888-481-2665**

PROMO JB9ND

NEW DIRECTIONS FOR YOUTH DEVELOPMENT
IS NOW AVAILABLE ONLINE AT WILEY INTERSCIENCE

What is Wiley InterScience?

Wiley InterScience is the dynamic online content service from John Wiley & Sons delivering the full text of over 300 leading scientific, technical, medical, and professional journals, plus major reference works, the acclaimed *Current Protocols* laboratory manuals, and even the full text of select Wiley print books online.

What are some special features of Wiley InterScience?

Wiley InterScience Alerts is a service that delivers table of contents via e-mail for any journal available on Wiley InterScience as soon as a new issue is published online.
Early View is Wiley's exclusive service presenting individual articles online as soon as they are ready, even before the release of the compiled print issue. These articles are complete, peer-reviewed, and citable.
CrossRef is the innovative multi-publisher reference linking system enabling readers to move seamlessly from a reference in a journal article to the cited publication, typically located on a different server and published by a different publisher.

How can I access Wiley InterScience?

Visit http://www.interscience.wiley.com

Guest Users can browse Wiley InterScience for unrestricted access to journal Tables of Contents and Article Abstracts, or use the powerful search engine.
Registered Users are provided with a *Personal Home Page* to store and manage customized alerts, searches, and links to favorite journals and articles. Additionally, Registered Users can view free Online Sample Issues and preview selected material from major reference works.
Licensed Customers are entitled to access full-text journal articles in PDF, with select journals also offering full-text HTML.

How do I become an Authorized User?

Authorized Users are individuals authorized by a paying Customer to have access to the journals in Wiley InterScience. For example, a university that subscribes to Wiley journals is considered to be the Customer. Faculty, staff, and students authorized by the university to have access to those journals in Wiley InterScience are Authorized Users. Users should contact their Library for information on which Wiley journals they have access to in Wiley InterScience.

ASK YOUR INSTITUTION ABOUT WILEY INTERSCIENCE TODAY!

Cultural**Agents**

Building Society Through Arts and Humanities

The mission of Cultural Agents is to promote the arts and humanities as social resources. We foster creativity and scholarship that measurably contribute to the education and development of communities worldwide. Identifying creative agents of change, reflecting on best practices, and inspiring their replication, we show that creativity sustains healthy democracies by developing the moral imagination and resourcefulness in citizens

Based at Harvard University, Cultural Agents brings together artists, educators, and community leaders in innovative collaborations that revitalize civic life both locally and internationally. Our activities feature workshops, conferences, TV programs, performances, exhibitions, and scholarly publications

Cultural Agents Initiative
Dept of African and African American Studies
Harvard University
Barker Center, 2nd Floor
12 Quincy Street Cambridge, MA 02138
e-mail: cultagen@fas.harvard.edu